Nice To Meet Your Husband Sister Martha

Margaret Connor Peifer

Nice to Meet Your Husband Sister Martha

Margaret Connor Peifer

Published by artpacks
535 22nd Street NE
Rochester, MN   55906
507·273·2529

Book and cover design by Virginia Woodruff
The text is set in Minion Pro and Blackjack
Photo layouts by Katie Gillen and Virginia Woodruff
Designed, printed, and bound in the United States of America

Connor Peifer, Margaret
Nice To Meet Your Husband Sister Martha
p.cm
ISBN 13: 978-0-9790247-2-6 (pbk)
ISBN 10: 0-9790247-2-2 (pbk)
1. Memoir
2. Religion
3. Cancer

To my beloved Jack and my loving family and friends

"I am a part of all that I have met."   — TENNYSON

Contents

Acknowledgments

Gail Hunter who taped and typed for a year and said, "do it."
Virginia Woodruff who planned and designed the book.
Cele Bona, friend and writer, who edited my first drafts.
Stephen Thornton and Sarah Stoll who typed the manuscript
and encouraged me.
Katie Gillen, graphic artist, who composed photo layouts.
Jack who has inspired me and supported me in every way.

Preface

My friend, Ruthie, is a great pianist. Whenever I sing along, she wrinkles her nose and says, "Well, Margie, you have volume and nerve." It is in this spirit that I present my story.

I was born in 1935 in Joliet, Illinois. It was the time of the Great Depression, but I was blessed with an extraordinary mom, dad, and brother.

I end the story of my 70 years living happily on a farm in Lincoln, Illinois. I am grateful for each year of my life and look forward to the future, because "the best is yet to be, the last of life for which the first was made." — BROWNING

Mom, Dad,
and I at
the convent

In 6th grade, S. Generosa
planted the seed for my
becoming a nun

One

Climbing Over The Wall

As a happily married woman of 70, I look back on the day I entered the convent as a major step in my life's journey. It was the time that I finally said in a public way that my life is about serving the Lord and His people.

I remember in sixth grade asking my mom how Daddy proposed. Hoping for a romantic story, I was disappointed when she said, "Well, we both sort of knew that we'd get married." It was a bit that way with the convent for me.

My sixth grade teacher, Sister Generosa OP, a Dominican Sister in a white habit, asked me one day right outside the classroom, "Margie, have you ever thought about being a sister?" I don't remember what I said, but I know that I was pleased that she had asked. In eighth grade, I signed up to take a test for a Dominican boarding school operated by the same sisters who taught at my school. I did not earn a scholarship, and we did not have money for the boarding school. That dream was short lived. Later I used to say, "If I were smart or rich, I would have been a Dominican."

The summer after my sophomore year in high school, I began studying at Grailville, a lay-religious community on a large farm outside of Cincinnati, Ohio. Started by a Dutch woman, it was something of a Catholic "back to the land" movement that prepared women for apostolic work in the church. I loved it. One day the director asked me if I wanted a scholarship to stay there longer. I remember feeling torn. I finally said aloud for the first time, "I think I want to become a sister."

Grailville was a commune of Catholic women, a sisterhood. Together, the women prayed and lived lives characterized by celibacy and modest poverty. I learned to pray the daily Psalms of The Divine Office, a prayer that monks, cloistered nuns, priests, and sisters say five times a day. The difference was that the Grailville women did these things a little more leisurely and creatively which got me in the spirit of saying the group prayers at night. The summer in Grailville was an important influence on my decision to become a nun.

It was my senior year in high school when I told Sister Clarice I wanted to apply to be a nun. She took me over to the big motherhouse, a large stone building on the other side of the campus. We walked down long halls lined with pictures of all the former Mothers Superior on our way to meet the current Mother Superior, Mother Immaculate Buckstegge. She was small and frail with a welcoming smile. Forty six years later, I would marry her nephew.

I remember getting the black trunk, black stockings, all the silly underwear, white nightgowns, and plain black shoes. I had to sew my number, 746, in red on every item, even my underwear that was so ugly that it looked like men's. I also recall the white button-down, long-sleeved shirts, also reminiscent of menswear. All this was very sobering.

On Sunday, September 7, 1953, I joined the convent. It was a sad day at the time. My girlfriend, Ruthie, stood on my front porch and sobbed when she came over to say goodbye. Ruthie was known for her humor, intelligence, and stoicism. I had never seen her cry, and it startled me. Was I never to see her again? I assured her that I would see her soon.

Driving away from my yellow home on McDonough Street with my family, I was filled with excitement and nostalgia. Charlie drove. Mom sat in the back with me. Each of us quietly tried to be brave.

Dad had reservations about my joining the sisterhood but was willing to let me try it.

The Motherhouse of the Sisters of St. Francis stood at the top of a hill only three miles from my home, but I knew that it would be six years before I would ever get back to McDonough Street.

When we arrived at 520 Plainfield Road, the four of us got out of the car and walked toward the long stairway. Dad and Charlie took my black trunk to a storage area. In contrast to our melancholy family, there was a happy group of sisters welcoming us at the top of the stairs. I said my final goodbye to my family. I cried, and my Dad gave me his handkerchief. My friend Cele bounded up the stairs at the last minute

COLLEGE OF SAINT FRANCIS, JOLIET, ILLINOIS

Motherhouse

SFA

Climbing over the Wall

746 *The day I entered the convent in 1953, Dad gave me his hankie to wipe my tears.*

My favorite spot at 621 McDonough Street

to give me a final hug. We stood nose to nose on opposite sides of the convent screen door, and she pleaded with me, "Don't do this."

We walked with the sisters to the postulancy, after I donned my black shoes, black cotton stockings, white cotton underwear and a black dress, cape, and veil. The room was large and had 16 desks lined up in pairs. Seats were assigned by age, and I was second oldest. Miss Ruth Marie, a woman who had left the convent earlier and returned, was number one and happy to be back. The younger members of the class had been in school together at the high school prep for three years, so it was a reunion for them after their summer vacation.

Our first group activity, as a new class, was to go to the chapel for prayer at 4:00 p.m. We were to walk in silence as partners, eyes cast down, with our hands folded under our capes. The "eyes cast down" or "custody of the eyes" helped us focus ourselves for prayer. It was the first convent practice I learned and one that I always found difficult. Our postulant mistress, Sister Zita, had to teach us these things quickly for the chapel was filled with the novices and professed sisters waiting for our entrance.

Then we ate with the novices. The dining room was divided so that the first and second year novices sat on one side of the room, and the newcomers sat together on the other side. We were not allowed to talk during dinner time, and a novice read scriptures out loud. Then at one point during the meal, the Superior would say "Benedicamos Domino," signaling we could talk. We quickly got into the routine and were put to work the next day.

I was starting college, and my job was helping the librarian.

During my sophomore year, my homeroom and English teacher was Sister Jean Paul who was tall and exciting. Although she was from Chicago, Sister Jean Paul spoke as though she had attended college in the East. She introduced us to Dorothy Day, the Catholic Worker Movement, and Grailville in Ohio. I respected her.

Sister Jean Paul left the community and became a laywoman before I entered. Her handwriting was a distinctive rolling print with a backhand slant. Her writing was on the library cards that I was holding in my new job. I was assigned to make new cards for the books that were on reserve. Many of the cards were full of names, and I was to rip them up and throw them away. I felt like I was desecrating Sister Jean Paul.

The wonderful part of the sisterhood was being in a commune of very intelligent, purposeful women. Long before the women's movement, nuns were feminists. In the 1950s, the nuns were the heads of

Open, O Lord, my lips to bless Thy holy name: cleanse my heart from all vain, foolish, and wandering thoughts; enlighten my understaning, enkindle my affections, and grant that I may recite this Office with devotion, so that I may be heard in the presence of Thy divine Majesty. Through Christ, our Lord. Amen.

O Lord, in union with that divine intention with which Thou, whilst on earth, didst Thyself praise God, I offer Thee this Hour.

4

hospitals, colleges, high schools, and grade schools. They held leadership roles that other women didn't.

I felt destined to be a nun. My Grandma Connor preached service for the less fortunate. She ran a Mission Club that raised money for Indian and Black Missions, and my mother had me help everyone in the neighborhood. I would go shopping for two ladies on the block and a third a few blocks away. Maybe, if I had been born 15 years later, I would have joined the Peace Corps. I thought about being a missionary sister, but someone told me they gave you shots *Climbing over* with a needle that was six inches long. With that in the back of my *the Wall* mind, I gave up the idea.

In 1953, working women were mainly nurses and teachers, and a few brave ones were doctors. There were no women bankers or engineers; women did not do these things at all.

I wanted to be a teacher, and when I entered the convent, I knew I could become one. Though I always knew that I would miss having babies, there was no question that I was going to be a nun, and nuns could not have babies. Also, I never knew how much I would miss men. The whole sexual side of me hadn't really hit me yet. When I entered the convent, I was simply drawn to the Sisters that were teachers. They were brilliant women in my mind.

My big fear was that I was leaving my mom with only my dad and brother to take care of her. I kept saying to Daddy and Charlie, "Are you sure this is OK that I go into the convent?" I'm sure my father felt that the convent was not the best place for me. But he was still proud to have me as a religious sister.

When I entered the convent, there was still a nun in our Franciscan community named Sister Martha, and the year I was postulant, she died. We didn't use our last names in the convent, so you had to pick a name that was not used in the community. The fact that Sister Martha died right while I was a postulant gave me the option of taking "Sister Martha" for my name.

I was born on the Feast of St. Martha, July 29, 1935, on a Wednesday, and my grandma always had her Martha Society meeting every Wednesday. I would become Sister Martha, which would honor my Grandma Connor and make sure my birthday was celebrated on the proper day, as in the convent, feast days, not birthdays, are celebrated. I got to celebrate my birthday and feast day together.

My first year in the convent was difficult but fun. I knew I was in the right place. I wanted to "Serve the Lord. Alleluia! Yes!"

Come Holy Spirit, fill the hearts of your faithful and kindle in them the fire of your divine love. Send forth thy Spirit and they shall be created. You shall renew the face of the earth.

O, God who by the light of the Holy Spirit, did instruct the hearts of the faithful, grant that by the same Holy Spirit we may be truly wise and ever enjoy His consolations. Through Christ Our Lord, Amen.

Mom, Dad, Grandpa
McCauley, and Charlie
on Charlie's first birthday

By my first birthday, the Depression was on and
Dad was working for the WPA (Works Progress
Administration and CCC (Civilian Conservation Corps)

6

Two

My First Family Of Faith

As I strove to create bonds with my new chosen family in the convent, I worked equally hard to deal with my homesickness for my birth family. I missed Mom, Dad, and Charlie every day, and I asked a sister one day how long these feelings last. When she said, "Oh, about two to three years," I thought, "I'll likely be dead by then."

I remember the first Saturday afternoon when we went upstairs to the tub rooms to take our weekly baths. I got soap in my eyes while washing my hair and couldn't call for my mom. I was so used to my mom being within hollering distance, and I started to cry. I told myself that was foolish.

Each member of my family seemed an outstanding human being. Though Mom wasn't good at cleaning, cooking or caring for my clothes, she was holy, smart, funny, and kind. She was a teacher. My dad was a steelworker, loyal to God and family. Charlie was a smart, young "Don Quixote" destined for politics.

My mom was born in Joliet, Illinois, in 1899. She was a nervous person and a romantic, and she loved to tell stories. If we were taking the bus downtown she would make up a story about someone on the bus. Once she said, "Do you see that lady with the red purse? She has a bloody knife in it." It was difficult because she was sick my entire life.

When I was about five years old Mom became pregnant. John Francis was born and spent his four months of life in the hospital.

One of my earliest memories was walking with my mom across the Jefferson Street Bridge that covered the Joliet canal, and up a hill to St. Joseph's Hospital to visit our baby, John Francis.

3rd Generation Friends

Our grandmothers were friends;
Our mothers were friends;

Aunt Rose with me, & Loretta McCarney with Loretta McCarney (Junior)

With Loretta at her wedding...
It was supposed to be private,
and I hadn't asked permission
from the Superior General
to be a Nun of Honor

As a novice,
sharing a moment
with Loretta
McCarney, Senior

Mom would go upstairs and visit the baby alone because I was only five, and the hospital would not allow me to visit. I remember sitting in the lobby and playing with the cigarette machine. This is the time I started in my mind to take care of my mom. On the day John Francis was to come home, my mom had all his baby clothes ready. Only then did the doctor tell my mom and dad that the baby needed more hospital care.

In the four months, Mom visited him every day. My dad worked shift work at the steel mill, and I imagine that he went to visit John before or after work. My brother, Charlie, was already in the sixth grade. Possibly He and Dad went with Mom on weekends.

John Francis died of Pneumonia. I still remember the wake. Every hour or so I would walk up and look at him. He was beautiful in a blue cotton outfit. He did not look like he was sick or dead, just a sweet sleeping baby.

Mom often went to daily mass, and sometimes she took me with her. At a mass after the baby's death, Mom came back from communion, and as she bowed her head and put her hands over her face to pray, I wiggled close to her and whispered, "Don't cry Mama!" It was in that moment that I designated myself as Mama's Helper. Dad and Charlie were caring, but I believed that I was the most supportive.

Later Mom would often say, "I should have just taken him home; he probably would have lived." She was always beating herself up over John's death. I really think my mom was sick from then on. My aunts would always tell me to be good to my mom, so I, from about age five or six, began to assume the role of caretaker.

Mom had been sickly as a child. I had heard stories of her falling off a horse when she was young. I think that she always had high blood pressure and a weak heart.

Right around the time of John Francis's death, I remember times when I felt embarrassed. We had great neighbors who were Norwegian and not Catholic. One day I was in their kitchen for the first time. I sat on a chair, and my neighbor washed my feet. I imagine that she washed my face and hands too, but all I remember thinking is, "Why is some other mommy washing me?"

Another embarrassing memory I have from this time is when my mom took me shopping downtown. On a top floor of an office building was a beauty school where Mom had my thick, curly hair washed and cut. The girl who cut my hair said to another beautician, "Wow, this hair is so greasy, look at my hands!" I felt so ashamed. I never blamed my mom because I knew that she was sick.

Rossi

JOLIET, ILL.

My First Holy Communion

My first communion picture was taken a few months after the
hair cut incident. I remember my mom taking my dress to the photo
studio in a box. The dress was white, cotton organdy, and so wrin-
kled that the photographer could only take my picture from the
waist up. The wrinkles still showed in the picture.

When I was about 11 years old my mom called her older sister,
Aunt Margaret, to come over because Mom was afraid she was

having a heart attack. An ambulance was called, and when the medics arrived with the stretcher, mom said, "I cannot be carried out. I'm scared!" Aunt Margaret scolded her, "Ann, lie down and be quiet!" I had never heard my mom being scolded and I felt badly.

After the flurry of activity as the ambulance pulled away carrying Mom, Charlie, and Aunt Margaret, I stood alone in our large empty house watching through a beveled glass panel on the side of our front door. I felt numb. I knew I had grown up fast.

My mom was in charge of getting an article to the Joliet Herald News every week about who was hosting my grandma's weekly Martha Society meeting. When I was seven years old my mother would put me on the bus to downtown at 7:30 in the morning. I learned to walk into the newspaper office, ask for the society editor, and put the article my mother had written on the editor's desk. I was really scared, but I was asked to do it, so I did! *My First Family of Faith*

My mother apparently thought that we did not deserve anything special. If one of my aunts sent me a box of taffy, my mother would say, "Well, let's give this to the neighbor because she is sick." She never thought that we should keep anything for ourselves. I know this is still with me today, and some friends warn me, "Please keep this," when giving me a gift.

My grandfather McCauley worked in a factory. He was a big man. His neck size was 22 inches. They weren't rich, but they were middle class. I think my grandfather was an alcoholic but was not a falling-down type because he always worked.

My grandmother McCauley was a small sweet being. I remember my mother telling me that at the table, the children were supposed to be really quiet, and once when my mom spoke out of turn, my grandfather slapped her. I was shocked. I always felt that my mother absorbed the worries in the family and that was why she was always nervous. I was really different than my mother. Although she was funny and creative, she was more retiring, and much quieter than I.

Because mom was sick our house was always a mess. The front room might be picked up. It was not horrible, but it wasn't right. I think that this had a big effect on my personality. If something was going to occur, I was always a nervous wreck because things were never prepared or ready. When my mother went back to teaching for a sick friend, I remember dressing myself for school.

This lack of preparedness made me extremely nervous if I was in charge of something. The fact that my mother was not on top of things wasn't because she was lazy. It was because she was unable.

My mom greatly influenced me. She was an English teacher, and I became an English teacher. She was a woman of prayer, very religious, and I became a nun and am still active in the church. She was very giving, and I think I have that gift. I believe that she brought me my greatest virtues and my greatest vices. The greatest vice would be not knowing how to clarify personal boundaries or teaching me how to take care of myself. I try to help others, and often I take on more than I can handle.

I always smile proudly when I talk about my dad. He was a character, totally loyal to his family, and a wonderful human being. He thought my brother and I were perfect. He was kind and loving to my mother even though she was sick a large part of their lives.

My dad was born in Lockport, Illinois in 1891. His family lived on what is now Connor Street. His father died when Dad was only 13. Grandma Connor made sure that my two aunts went to high school and college. However, she sent my dad to work in the mill at age 13, so he never went to high school. It seemed to hold him back. He worked at the Joliet Steel Mill on and off his entire life. He was in the army for a while, and after he married my mom, he tried to start two stores. Unfortunately, he did not have success with the stores, so he went back to what he knew best – the steel mill.

My dad had a tough life. He stood making hot rods in a furnace, and shift work meant that he never worked the same hours two weeks in a row. He never missed a day of work, but he never got ahead at work either. I never could figure out why. Was it a lack of education or his personality? I always felt sorry for dad because I felt he really didn't like the mill. He was on relief during the Depression and worked in the government programs, WPA and CCC camps. I think this was very hard on my father, but he never complained.

My father was extremely proud of my brother, Charlie. Charlie was a good athlete, and my father would go on the bus to Chicago to watch his football games. Can you imagine this little Joliet Catholic high school playing football with the big schools of Chicago? They generally got crushed. If Joliet Catholic High School made even one touchdown, we considered it a victory. To this day, Charlie talks about how good our dad was to him.

A strong memory of my dad is of him reading the Chicago Tribune and going off to work. I was a little scared of Dad. He was deaf and loud, and my mom taught me at a very young age how to avoid confronting him. After we went shopping, for example, we would come in the back door and hide some of the purchases. Mom would say that she would show daddy later.

I always knew my dad loved my mom though I never saw great physical affection between them. We would each kiss Dad good-bye when he left for work. We would say, "God bless you and bring you safe home." I saw the tender side of my dad when my mom was really sick. When she had to go to a nursing home, Dad would go over to feed her every day.

When Charlie became a Will County judge, he officiated at weddings in our home. Initially, my father thought this was terrible, so when the people who wanted to get married came to our house, he would go visit a neighbor or something to show he wanted no part of it. After a while, he came to love it, and he would welcome the brides and grooms in and put a romantic record on.

My dad loved politics and was very loyal to the Republican Party. He always said, "I was a Democrat until I learned to read." He would sit and talk politics to anyone who was interested. He would make up things like, "The Pete McCarthy's Soup Kitchen gave us an extra dessert today," in front of people who did not know him. I get my sense of humor from both my mom and dad.

When my mom died, I had already been in the convent more than ten years. I was stationed in Joliet, so I was allowed to go home every weekend to help with washing and cleaning at Dad's house. These were pleasant visits. He was very happy when I could come. He was also very deaf, so I had to almost scream when I talked to him. We watched TV together on Saturday nights. "Mannix" was a favorite show.

One of my favorite stories about my dad was when my brother Charlie got married. My brother and I took care of two aunts, an uncle, and one second cousin, Aunt Kit. Charlie became her guardian. Aunt Kit was a very tiny woman who was fashionably dressed and wore pretty hats. She was very different from the rest of the Connor family, who all dressed simply and were large. When Aunt Kit got sick Charlie took her to a senior home in Joliet, and met Alice, a mother of three, who looked like Debbie Reynolds. She was in her thirties and just divorced. Alice directed the nursing home that Charlie chose for Aunt Kit, and coincidentally Alice's parents also ran a nursing home that happened to be where our mom stayed. Alice's mom told Alice to give this Charlie fellow a good look because he was a good man, handsome, a judge, and a bachelor.

Charlie was late paying Aunt Kit's bill, so Alice asked him to stop in for a cup of coffee, and that's how it all got started.

One day, Charlie and Alice were at the nursing home discussing Aunt Kit when she looked up from the bed and said, "You two would make a good pair."

They began dating, but since Alice was divorced, Charlie was uncomfortable. They dated a while and soon became very serious. Charlie really wanted to marry Alice, but he hesitated because of his faith. Then they started to see if there was a way to get an annulment, and they began the lengthy process. After a year, Alice finally said, "Here take the ring back, I'm not going to marry you if this is going to go on and on." Charlie thought about this for a while and decided that he did not want to live without Alice, so they set a date for the wedding. They decided to get married by a justice of the peace and it would be on Holy Saturday.

I spoke to my friend, a priest, about the wedding because I really wanted to go but also had concerns. My friend said, "Your brother isn't leaving the church, the church is just leaving your brother."

I then talked to Dad and said, "Dad, I would really like to go to Charlie's wedding, but I'm not going to go and leave you home alone. If you really don't feel up to going to the wedding, I will stay home with you." My dad thought about this and decided to come to the wedding. We drove together in a station wagon – a bride in a veil, the groom in a tuxedo, the three children, an old man and a nun. At the wedding and at the small reception, I was the proudest I have ever been of my father. An old saying states: "It is one thing for a father to be a father when your children are making you feel good, but it takes a great dad to be there when you are not so proud."

Thanks to my parents, being a postulant was easy for me. I had the spirituality of my mom, the orderliness of my dad, and from Charlie, the confidence to "Just do it!"

My dad was very different from my mom. A veteran of World War I he was quite regimented. I actually enjoyed the military aspect of being a postulant; making our beds with square corners, dressing in a uniform of black and white, and polishing our black oxfords every Saturday. I was comfortable with this sense of routine.

Both my parents were strong in their Catholic faith but were at opposite ends of the spectrum. My mother was a romantic Catholic, while my dad focused on the Catholic rules. For example, my mom tried to go to mass and communion everyday. My dad felt that he was a sinner and that the only time he could go to communion was a Sunday following a Saturday confession. If he went to confession on Saturday, we had to be very good because he felt that if he lost his temper with us, he wouldn't be worthy to go to communion. My mother thought communion was to strengthen us, while my dad thought that the Eucharist was a reward. Funny that growing up, I never felt like we were a good Catholic family because my brother was not an altar boy, my father was never an usher, and my mother did not belong to the Altar and Rosary Society. Also we never went to mass as a family. I went to children's mass or later the choir mass, while Mom went to an early mass. Dad went to a late mass. I'm sure that Charlie went sometime.

My First Family of Faith

Another thing I remember about my father was that when there was a Holy Day of Obligation and the day fell on a weekday, my father would go to mass at 5:00 a.m. at St. Mary's downtown. He had to walk to the church, which was about four or five miles, and then walk two miles to work. The buses weren't running that early and we did not own a car. His faith was severely tested at the death of his namesake, John Francis. These days were some of the hardest times for all of us.

Growing up, I was always proud to say, "Charlie Connor is my big brother." Charlie was born in Joliet, Illinois in 1928. When I was born, Charlie was six and a half years old. He was not really a big part of my early life, because when I was five or six it seemed he was always down the street playing with the Kanes who lived across from West Park and had seven boys and eventually one girl. Charlie considered himself a Kane. As we got older, we got closer. Charlie was born during the Depression and remembers being very poor. I have a picture of my brother taken when he was about three or four years old and he looks like a war refugee. I really never knew what it was like to be that poor because by the time I was two or three, dad had a steady job in the steel mill.

I grew up knowing Charlie was very smart. Mom always said that Charlie never had to study because he was so smart. I think that probably made me try harder and be a little more humble. It actually took me a while to figure out that I had a good mind.

I remember when Charlie was 11 or 12, he took an achievement test. When he received the scores, his weren't the highest. My mother was sure that there was some mistake if my brother was not number one, so she went to his classroom and asked his Dominican teacher to check the official scores. I do not remember the end of the confrontation. I believe the sister was correct.

Margaret Mary "Muggs" Connor, now Sister Martha, at age 3, and her brother, Charlie, now Joliet's mayor, at age 10.

Charlie's idea of a birthday card to me

When Charlie was nineteen and a junior in college, I remember my mom and I went to Milwaukee to find him a dorm room. He had attended St. Joe's College in Rennsalear, Indiana for two years, and was transferring to Marquette in Milwaukee for engineering. We ended up looking at boarding houses for college men. That was a big deal for me because I had never traveled with my mother out of town. My mother was not feeling well, and I sprained my ankle. I remember a handsome, young medical student taking care of my ankle and making me feel special. We did get Charlie a room.

When Charlie was in college, we began spending more time together. When he came home for holidays we started to do a few things. I do not think that either my mom or dad was ever that excited about Christmas. In junior high, I remember Charlie and I would go out to get our tree a few days before Christmas. On Christmas day we went to Grandma Connor's house for the actual holiday dinner but we started taking responsibilities for our home celebration. I always liked my brother's friends. After Charlie graduated from

16

Charlie as Senior Class President

1946

My First
Family
of Faith

CONNOR
for
CONGRESS

Lost!

CONNOR
Circuit Judge

Won!

Charlie as
Judge

... always a winner with me!

Marquette, he had an engineering degree and worked in down town Chicago for about a year. After that he went into the service. I remember standing in tears at the station as he left.

We thought he was going to Japan or someplace far away. He got lucky, though, and he trained at Ft. Leonard Wood in Missouri, and then he was stationed in Toledo, Ohio. After that he made the last-minute decision to attend law school. Charlie wanted to go to De Paul University because it was a Catholic University, but because he had registered late, he did not get in. He ended up going to the University of Chicago.

Charlie was always a big part of my life, and he still is. Basically for me he was the perfect big brother. Although we did argue, and he scared me sometimes, he was still my one and only big brother, and I loved him dearly.

A favorite story of ours, which my brother told at my wedding, is about my excessive talking. My grandma lived about four or five miles away on the south side of town. One day Charlie and I decided to walk to see her. I was about 12 and Charlie was about 18 or 19. I started talking to Charlie along the way. As we walked along Charlie said to himself, "I wonder if Muggs will ever notice if I don't talk." He said I talked during the entire walk to grandma's house. He finally told me when we arrived, that he had never said one word. I had not noticed.

While working as a principal, a parent who was in charge of a parent club called to tell me that he had been in rehabilitation for alcoholism. He wanted to come to my office because he had taken some funds from the club. I got scared because I was supposed to be in charge of all the affairs at the school, yet I had no idea that he had taken any money. I believed that I had let the school down, so I quickly called Charlie, who was chief judge at that time in Joliet. I said, "Charlie, something has happened, and this gentleman is coming to my office – what should I have him sign? What should I do?"

The first thing Charlie told me was to be kind, and I was so glad he told me this because the man was really upset. He was a wonderful parent and paid back the money. The parent was humiliated, and the best thing I could do was be kind, which I was. Charlie was a good lawyer and judge, but he still led with his heart and made me proud.

As a postulant in The Sisters of St. Francis of Mary Immaculate, I felt that my family had given me the right stuff to make it.

Three

Be A Cheerful Giver

There were definite stages to becoming a Sister of St. Francis of Mary Immaculate. During stage one, I applied and was accepted. Stage two was a year long postulancy from September to August. The "stage two" year, although I was homesick, was fun. It was a cross between voluntarily joining the army and a first year away at college.

During the first year, I got up to a bell at 5:00 a.m.

We had to be organized to quickly bathe and dress.

We pinned a small black veil to a white celluloid band. We had two veils, and the one that was not being used was placed between two thick cardboards and slipped under our mattresses. We pinned small white cuffs on our long-sleeved black serge dresses. Every item of clothing had numbers on them for laundry purposes. One morning after I was dressed, I noticed that my number, 746, was showing on the outside of my white cuff. I quickly put white toothpaste over it to hide it, so that I would be on time for morning prayer at 5:20.

We each had a cell, a monastic term for small bedroom, consisting of a bed and a night stand separated by curtains, and we had sponge baths from Sunday through Friday. On Saturday we bathed in a tub.

Our postulant mistress, Sister Zita, slept in an alcove in our dorm, and it was her first year as postulant mistress. She smiled easily. We had three superiors that year – the Superior of the Congregation, Mother Immaculate; the superior of the house, Sister Edith; and our postulant mistress, Sister Zita. I was well trained for this matriarchal society because that was how I was raised.

Confirmation Ceremony, June 1954
I'm blocked by Margaret Sheehan,
who is two over from Sr. Zita, our
Postulant Mistress.

Sarah Jane (Bannon) Connor:
Family Matriarch & President
of the Martha Society

Growing up, Grandma Connor ruled the roost. She was the head honcho, very independent, quite religious, and very much a leader. She never complained, even about the weather, because, "That is the weather God gave you for the day, so don't complain and never brag." Her idea of service was quiet and not preachy.

Grandma Connor is the main reason I am so reluctant to talk about my life. Grandma Connor thought that if kids were praised too much, they would get big heads. I knew my grandma thought the world of Charlie and me, but we couldn't brag around her. If my aunts came over and my mom had my hair curled really pretty or if they complimented me on my new dress, Grandma would always say to them, "Don't do that, you are going to spoil her." So you weren't allowed to praise anyone out loud around Grandma. I learned that I shouldn't talk about myself.

My grandma was larger-than-life and an organizer. Every Wednesday I would go over to my grandma's house and help her set up card tables for the weekly card game. The "Martha Society" was a group of ladies who would get together once a week to play cards and collect money for the missions. The two missions they helped were a Native American mission in North Dakota and an African American mission in Alabama. When they were younger they would sew clothes for the children at the missions, but as they got older they would just play cards and collect money. It was also my job each week to put out the cigar box that was covered in paper, with a slot cut in the middle for money. It said, "God loves a cheerful giver." You always had to put money in Grandma's box. *Be a Cheerful Giver*

Grandma Connor lived on the opposite side of Joliet from me. My family did not have a car, but there was a bus that ran all the way through downtown to where Grandma lived. When I was about five years old, my mom put me on the bus alone, and Uncle Matt helped me get me off the bus. I don't remember paying because I must have been underage. I would sit right next to the driver until Uncle Matt helped me off the bus. Then I would go visit Grandma. I remember my brother making fun of me because I was so scared the first time. My brother said, "I'll tell Grandma you don't love her."

The Connor family did not seem to believe in procreation. I had two maiden aunts who were teachers and my Uncle Matt who was a bachelor; they all lived with Grandma Connor. My father was the only one in the Connor family who got married and by the time my dad had me he was 43. Grandma Connor's only grandchildren were my brother and I. I was my Grandma Connor's first and only granddaughter and by the time I knew her, she was already 80 years old.

Grandma Connor physically reminded me of a white Aunt Jemima. She was a large woman and every time I came to see her she would be sitting in the same tan wicker chair at the far end of this large front room. She was the first thing I would see when I came through the door. She wore a little bun on her head, and although she was 80 years old, she was a mighty woman.

"Life gives you pretty much what you give it. She gives beauty to those who try to add to her beauty. She gives happiness to those who share their happiness with her. She gives, even, love to those who love her. But these are very, very few. Almost all of us have a capacity for being loved. But few of us have a capacity for loving."

Gram's caretakers – Uncle Matt, me, Aunt Rose, and Aunt Grace

Grandma Connor was almost blind, but she still loved to play cards. She had macular degeneration. We went to Grandma's home every Sunday night where we would play Euchre. She would hold the cards up very close to her eyes so she could see. I don't remember grandma ever scolding me or complimenting me. She wasn't demanding. I guess my uncle and my parents did anything that needed to be done. It is funny to think about now. She had a profound influence on me, though it was not an intimate relationship. She was my grandma, and I tried to please her. The closest thing I can remember to a relationship with her was when I used to read her articles and short stories out of the Catholic magazine called *The Extension Society*. I was reading Grandma a story when I was seven or eight, and it was talking about people hugging and kissing. I was so worried that it would shock Grandma. I remember trying to protect her from the story.

I think my grandma might have been a bit "anti-men." As a very young girl she had worked in homes as a maid. This may have been an unpleasant experience because she didn't appear to want her girls to work for others. The girls went to college but the boys only finished grade school. I think another reason was because my Aunt Rose and Aunt Grace were teachers and in those days you couldn't get married unless you gave up your job. Grandma didn't want that, so men were discouraged around the place. Maybe I got that sentiment too, but it wore off eventually.

Be a Cheerful Giver

When I was a freshman in high school, one of the Sisters at St. Francis Academy gave us a book to read in English class called *Mr Blue* by Myles Connolly. It was an imaginative book, and I fell in love with it. When I was a junior in high school I started to read it to Grandma on Sunday visits. I was halfway through the book the week my grandma died. I found out one morning when my mother woke me for school and said, "Honey, go in and offer Dad sympathy because Grandma died last night." I still own a copy of *Mr Blue,* and I always think of Grandma when I see it.

Grandma Connor is the only person I have ever seen laid out in the Franciscan habit of The Third Order of St. Francis, who was not a sister or priest. She was a loyal member of The Third Order and was adamant about being buried in that humble garb. This was the same robe that I received in August of my postulancy year.

My main goal that first year was to demonstrate that I could follow the modified lifestyle of a vowed sister. My secondary goal was to attend college. Being outside the cloister at college was strange because I'd see high school classmates in the hall at school, and I was cautioned not to speak at length with them. I think I did much smiling and walking quickly. Even more difficult was not speaking to the sisters who taught me in high school. I saw them in chapel and dinner times, but only greetings were allowed.

At the end of the first year, we received the brown habit and white veil of a novice. June and July were filled with preparation. We sent official invitations to our family and friends for our August

Reception when we would receive our sister names and brown habits. We learned to sew "coifs" – this was a white cotton head-gear, which covered our hair. We placed this on our head to cover our hair, then put on a white celluloid band around that and we pinned on the white veil. The coifs encircled our faces. There were three basic shapes: A, B, and C, depending on the shape of your face. I was an amateur seamstress. My partner became tired of seeing me grimace as I tried to sew the coifs and offered to sew them for me. I'm sure this was without the permission of the postulant mistress. However, I did hem my new brown habit.

Jesus, meek and humble of heart, make my heart like unto thine.

Early in July, we tried on the white organdy bridal dresses that were kept upstairs in the big brown cabinets. The dresses were worn only one day a year – the day that a postulant became a novice. The seamstress sister took us for fittings, one at a time. The dresses were cut in an A-line pattern with a touch of lace around the neck and cuffs. We also wore a simple white veil and no jewelry.

The ceremony took place on August 13, 1954, in St. Raymond's Cathedral in Joliet. Leading up to this day we went on a ten-day re-treat led by a Franciscan priest. On the actual day, we processed from the mother house three blocks to the cathedral in a single file, with our eyes lowered. A cross-bearer led the procession of twenty postulants and twenty-second year novices in white nun veils. The second-year novices made simple vows that day, which lasted three years. They also received their black veil and crucifix.

The religious ceremony was satisfying, very formal and very beau-tiful. Bishop McNamara presided, and the Sisters' choir had prac-ticed the music all summer. The cathedral was filled with family, friends, and as many sisters as could attend – at least 300. Soon each class was called to the altar, and the brown habits were blessed and given to us in a bundle. We also received our new names. I was to be Sister Mary Martha. This was the name I would have for the next thirty-six years. After that, we left the sanctuary and went to a large room where we had all our hair cut off. We then changed into our brown habits and white veils.

A great celebration followed at our spacious campus back at the mother house. As we processed back, we found many large circles of lawn chairs waiting. We each had our own circle for visiting with our family and friends.

I was now Sister Martha, and overwhelmed with joy. Everything prior to this day had converged. I would carry on Grandma's mission by working for the poor, not complaining, and giving cheerfully.

Margaret - Margie

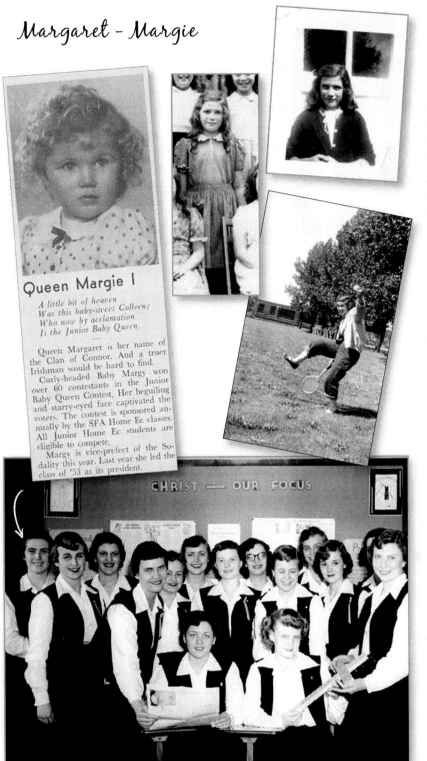

Queen Margie I

*A little bit of heaven
Was this baby-sweet Colleen;
Who now by acclamation
Is the Junior Baby Queen.*

Queen Margaret is her name of the Clan of Connor. And a truer Irishman would be hard to find. Curly-headed Baby Margy won over 60 contestants in the Junior Baby Queen Contest. Her beguiling and starry-eyed face captivated the voters. The contest is sponsored annually by the SFA Home Ec classes. All Junior Home Ec students are eligible to compete.

Margy is vice-prefect of the Sodality this year. Last year she led the class of '53 as its president.

Cry out with joy to the Lord, all the earth. Serve the Lord with gladness. Come before him, singing for joy.

Know that He, the Lord, is God. He made us, we belong to Him. We are his people, the sheep of His flock.

Go within His gates, giving thanks. Enter His courts with songs of praise. Give thanks to Him and bless His name.

Indeed, how good is the Lord, eternal His merciful love. He is faithful from age to age.

PSALM 100

Rosemary & Sally, editors of The Focus, the school newspaper, pass the journalism cross to the new editors

*My class-
mates before
the ceremony*

Me

26

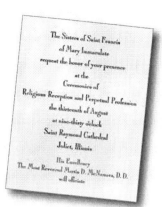

The Sisters of Saint Francis
of Mary Immaculate
request the honor of your presence
at the
Ceremonies of
Religious Reception and Perpetual Profession
the thirteenth of August
at nine-thirty o'clock
Saint Raymond Cathedral
Joliet, Illinois

His Excellency
The Most Reverend Martin D. McNamara, D.D.
will officiate

My Classmates and The McCauley Clan

My year of cloister began on that Sunday in August, 1954. It was a full day of celebration, and I became Sister Mary Martha. Early the next day another novice and I were assigned to laundry duty. I stood feeding wet sheets into a steaming industrial sized mangle. On the other side, two other novices collected the pressed sheets and folded them.

As I mentioned, our convent veil was pinned to a celluloid band which we placed on our forehead and held in the back with elastic. The combination of the heat of the gigantic mangle, the hot August temperature, the brown woolen habit, and the celluloid band was horrendous. I kept thinking, "Can't we take all this stuff off while we're working?" Standing dripping wet, I realized the celebration was over and my novitiate had begun. As with other adjustments, it symbolized the sacrifice of being a "soldier of Christ" – a good Franciscan sister. My goal was always clear and I was very willing.

The biggest sacrifice was that we could not see our parents, relatives, or friends for one full year. This discipline was to keep us focused on our new Franciscan family. We had all our college classes in the novitiate, so we no longer went next door to the college.

Our days were full. Sister Raphael was a tall sister who was always enthusiastic. She taught us Gregorian chant, which is the music created by the early Benedictine Monks. The chant was used at masses and in the recitation of the Divine Office. These special prayers, largely psalms, were chanted and prayed every three hours in monasteries of monks and cloistered sisters. The romantic in me was thrilled at the idea of monks and sisters leaving their cells to gather

Becoming Sister Martha

in the chapel for Matins – the midnight psalms, and then at 3 a.m., 6 a.m., and throughout the day. As Franciscans we prayed Lauds, the morning psalms, at 6 a.m., and Vespers, the evening psalms at 6:30 p.m., but did not rise during the night to pray.

Teaching Gregorian chant was a passion of Sister Raphael, and her appreciation was infectious as we learned the chants. Once we were novices, we said the Divine Office, as it was a requirement

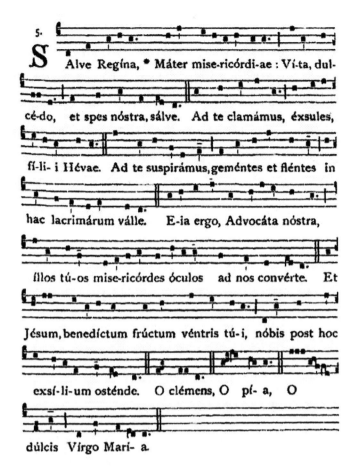

Salve regina, mater misericordiae,	Hail holy queen, mother of mercy,
Vita dulcedo et spes nostra salve.	Hail our life, our sweetness and our hope.
Ad te clamamus, exsules filii hevae.	To you do we cry poor banished children of Eve,
Ad te suspiramus gementes et flentes,	To you do we send up our sighs,
in hac lacrimarum valle.	mourning and weeping in this valley of tears.
Eia ergo advocata nostra,	Turn then, most gracious advocate
illos tuos misericordes oculos ad nos converte	your eyes of mercy toward us.
Et Jesum benedictum fructum ventris tui	And after this, our exile,
nobis post hoc exsilium ostende.	Show us the fruit of your womb, Jesus
O clemens, o pia, o dulcis Virgo Maria.	O clement, O loving, O sweet Virgin Mary.

like daily mass and meditation. The second-year novices led the Office prayers for the sisters at the chapel.

One day I was "Miss Margaret Mary" and the next day I was "Sister Martha." I loved hearing my new name and enjoyed addressing my classmates by theirs. My high school classmate, Shirley, was now Sister Josette. A quiet sister named Mary Alice became Sister Maristelle. During the novitiate our class size was 15.

Angel of God, My guardian dear, to whom His love commits me here, ever this day be at my side, to light and guard, to rule and guide. Amen

1940
Rosie, Me,
Mary Lou

Then & Now

1995
Rosie,
Me,
Mary
Lou

I grew up with fourteen cousins, so 15 was a comfortable number for me. As cousins, we called ourselves The McCauley Clan. My mom had three sisters who grew up in Forest Park, a part of Joliet on the east side of the city. All four sisters married within about five years of each other and immediately started their families. We all lived in Joliet, not too far from each other. Together, Margaret, Ann, Katherine, and Rose had 15 children. Most were born between 1927 and 1940 in the heart of the Depression.

Three out of the four sisters married gruff, crabby Irish husbands. *My Classmates and the McCauley Clan* The youngest, Aunt Rose married Frank who was a handsome, smiling Italian. The four sisters talked to each other on the phone frequently. Aunt Margaret was the oldest, and she and my mom never missed a day of talking on the phone.

Grandma and Grandpa McCauley died very early, but the girls and their families continued to get together for picnics, Christmas exchanges, and many birthday parties. Their only brother, Hugh, died at age 12 of diphtheria, after swimming in Spring Creek near Forest Park.

When my cousin Betty died in the 1990s, I spoke at her funeral. I said, "We were so close, I used to think it was solely because we loved each other so much. But today, I realize it was also because we were all poor and relied on each other." It truly was both.

Each of my mother's sisters had a specialty. Aunt Margaret was a seamstress and a baker, and served sugar cookies at every gathering. My mom was an old-fashioned country school teacher and tutored about half of us through the years. Aunt Katherine was a nurse and was the first to graduate from St. Joseph School of Nursing in Joliet; so we had someone to call when we got hurt. Aunt Rose was the youngest and the prettiest according to her sisters. She was a professional secretary and could handle any business situation. I always felt that we were ready for any exigency.

Growing up, there was always a first communion, graduation, or a birthday party to attend. My cousin Mary Lou got married in 1954, right before I entered the convent. That was the only wedding I attended for over 25 years because as nuns we couldn't attend such family functions. My cousin Pat Reardon stopped by the convent after her ceremony. My other cousin Pat Borio did the same thing. I was thrilled to see them. We treated each other like blood sisters. Later, when such regulations were changed, I actually attended my cousin Kay Borio's wedding and Charlie's.

Good Friends ...
McCauley Women

Mary Kay & family
hosted my 70th
birthday party

My cousins &
I at the party

The McCauley Clan

100 Years of Family Picnics

My Classmates and the McCauley Clan

Look what Patrick & Abigail and then Margaret, Ann, Catherine, and Rose began

With my mother's sisters

The Connor Women - Gram, Aunt Grace, Aunt Rose,
Me, & Mom....Aunt Margaret in the background

I had many
cousins as
playmates
Sitting here
with Mary Lou
in the McCauley
front yard

McCauley cousins
visit us in Lincoln

Center stage with Jack behind - next page

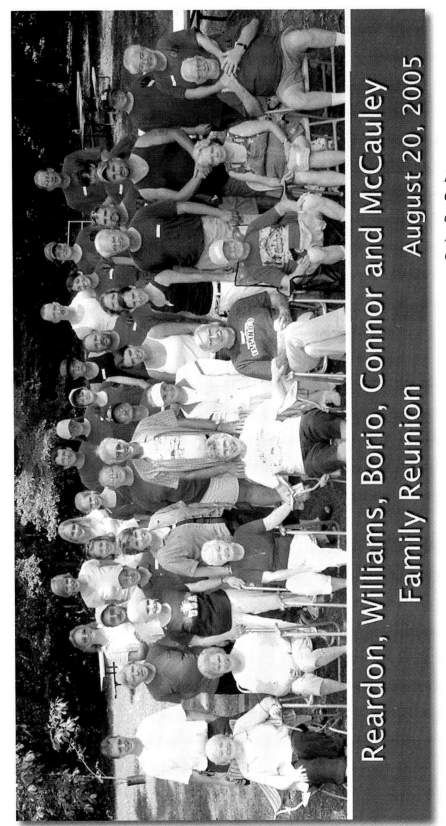

Reardon, Williams, Borio, Connor and McCauley
Family Reunion
August 20, 2005

My Classmates and the McCauley Clan

35

Ann's daughter,
McCauley Rose

Liam, Delia Rose, and
Declan Brennan

This extended family still gets together, though all of the first generation is gone. Aunt Rose died at age 93 in 1999, and my mom was born in 1899, so the McCauley girls had a great run. That was how I began a few words at the funeral mass for Aunt Rose. Three first cousins have also died – Danny, Betty, and Ray.

Pat Borio's daughters, Mary Kay and Anne, had a big party for women and children cousins for my 70th birthday. We had McCauley cousins present from the ages of eight weeks to 75 years old.

My cousins also helped Charlie run for public office, which he did four times. His friend Jack Kane, our cousin Tommy, and other cousins put campaign signs in yards. Cousin Rosemary headed up the

Mary Kay's daughter, Ali

Jeffrey

Maureen, Christine and sons

writing campaigns, and other cousins pitched in, along with good friend Ann Kane. I think Tommy finally suggested that Charlie stop with the "politicking" saying, "We're too old for this!" He ran four times and won twice, once for judge and then for mayor.

Another example of how our family helped each other was when I was principal of St. Francis Academy, and we were having a style show for the alumnae. When I arrived at the Renaissance Center where the style show was to be held, the runway looked awful. The ramp the women had to walk down was made of ugly-looking boards. I was sure a model would get a heel stuck and fall down. At 9:00 the morning of the show, I called my cousin Francis Borio, in the

*My first Mother Superior,
Jack's aunt!*

*A card made for me by
Sister Carolyn
St. Francis convent*

Aunt Rose with me as a postulant!

carpet business, for help. He came right over, looked at the situation, and left to find carpet to fix our problem. By 1:00 we were ready to open. The women walked down a beautiful red carpet.

In families, people get labels without their consent. Among the cousins, Rosemary was considered the beauty. In our novitiate the beauty was Sister Carolyn. The intellectual was Sister Alfred Marie – and in our family, the intellectual one was my brother, Charlie. The ladylike model would be Mary Fran, cousin – and Sister Mercedes, classmate. And in both groups I may have been known as an organizer. People always tell me I like being the boss. *My Classmates and the McCauley Clan*

First-year novitiate was definitely basic training. We focused on learning to pray and studying our rules and history. The class on "congregation history" began with the stories of St. Francis and St. Clare. St. Francis of Assisi attracted thousands to his way in the 13th century. He followed Christ quite literally – renouncing all the privileges to which he was born. He prayed, preached, begged, and lived in community. When women were interested in following Francis, with St. Clare as the leader, the Poor Clares were established. They centered on prayer and lived in a cloister, which is a convent that is a self-contained community. Although they planted gardens and did self-sustaining work, their main work was to pray; in this way, they were not like the followers of St. Francis, who begged and preached out in the world. St. Clare was not allowed on the public streets so could only reach others through conversations at the cloister gate.

Our community was part of the Third Order of Franciscans – lay people and religious. The First Order was the men Franciscans. The Second Order was the cloistered sisters known as "Poor Clares." Our sisters, known as the "Joliet Franciscans" was one of hundreds of communities of sisters founded by holy women in the United States during the 19th century.

The Joliet Franciscans were started in the 1860s by Father Pamfilio and Sister Alfred Moes. Mother Alfred Moes came to Joliet and founded our religious order and began a school in 1865, which was St. Francis Academy for girls of all ages – kindergarten through high school. Other women were drawn to her mission of education for German immigrants, and within ten years there were one hundred sisters.

In the late 1800s, Mother Alfred and a small group of sisters began a mission in Rochester, Minnesota. After a devastating tornado, Mother Alfred said to Dr. Mayo, "We need a hospital here. If I build it, will you and your sons staff it?" Dr. Mayo thought that in this city of mainly Protestants, Mother Alfred would not be able to achieve this. She did, however, and thus began the story of the Mayo brothers at St. Mary's Hospital.

For unknown reasons, the Cardinal of Chicago wanted Mother Alfred to return to Joliet immediately and threatened to dissolve her relationship with Joliet, which he did. In the 1950s, when we studied our history, Mother Alfred was named but not emphasized. There was a feeling that we had been abandoned.

The Second Vatican Council in the 1960s stressed looking at our roots. So by the 70s and 80s, we were having an annual "Mother Alfred Day." We are very connected to the Rochester Franciscans now, and extremely proud of Mother Alfred convincing Dr. Mayo and his sons to staff St. Mary's.

In the novitiate, in addition to the Divine Office and congregation history, we learned to prepare for our morning meditation, to appreciate the part silence played in our lives, and to choose reading materials that helped in our religious development. Thomas Merton was my favorite spiritual writer.

A community practice was introduced called "Chapter of Faults." Each Friday both classes of novices met. We stood in a circle at our desks. We prayed psalms together and then there was a time in which an individual novice could kneel and "acknowledge a fault." These were faults against our convents rules. People would kneel and say, "I came late to chapel this week," or, "I broke two plates while washing dishes." Often the penance was to say five "Our Fathers" privately or publicly.

If it were to be public, the novice would kneel with arms extended upwards and quietly say the assigned prayers while we were eating. The novice would kneel below the crucifix, which hung at the front of the dining room. I don't remember having to do this, but I must have. It was embarrassing but rather routine. In fact, if at any time the novice mistress corrected us, we were to kneel down immediately. I do remember doing that.

I used to share a "Chapter of Faults," a book of psalms, with Sister Mary Jean. Occasionally when we held the book together we had to stifle laughter as my large thumb set next to her unusually thin one. It was as if I were sharing the book with a child. I accepted "Chapter of Faults" and kneeling when corrected as part of the training. None of this angered or upset me.

Our cloistered year was 1954, a year that the church honored Mary in a special way. It was referred to as The Marian Year. The diocese planned a large celebration in her honor at the Joliet Football stadium. We were to go in buses and participate. As I got off the bus, I was startled to see my dad and brother standing by the gate. I hurried past as they greeted me. I caught up with an older sister and told her what happened. I actually thought that my seeing my family would cancel my novitiate.

The silence, study, and routine of those twelve months did accomplish specific goals. I prayed more easily, got closer to my classmates, and understood better the tradition, history, and practices of the Joliet Franciscans.

Our second year novitiate had a much different tempo as we could leave the cloister. We went back to college and resumed quarterly visits with family and friends. Sister Anacleta, our novice mistress, prepared us to take the vows of poverty, chastity, and obedience. These vows would be taken for three years only. After vows we would be assigned to a mission, the place where we would live and teach for the coming year.

As I look back, I think Sister Anacleta felt like a parent whose son or daughter was soon to be married. She wanted us to be ready for any situation. Sister would discuss differences between convents. If we were assigned to a large convent, much of the routine would be the same. But if it were a small one, we would participate in the cooking and other tasks, which might change the schedule. She emphasized the fact that mission life would be very different from novitiate life. I remember thinking, "What could be so different? Do we turn into different people?"

I questioned Sister Anacleta on this, but I think she thought it was better not to be too specific. While on mission, we were cautioned not to be too friendly with anyone. We were warned not to have long conversations with priests and janitors. This was before there were many laymen or women on the teaching staff. In the summer months before we took first vows, we had courses by great teachers in our congregation on how to teach phonics, how to keep discipline, and how to teach art. We were scared but ready!

On August 12, 1956, it was our turn for the profession ceremony which we had participated in as postulants. I was nervous but happy. We made an eight-day retreat, practiced our parts in the ceremony, and felt ready to make our temporary vows. We then donned our black veils, received our silver cross, and finally left for our mission. We returned to Joliet nine months later, veterans of teaching and convent experience.

Teaching...

St. Jude
School
Staff
1956-57

I was sent to
this convent
in the coun-
try because I
had a driver's
license. I drove
the Superior.
She sat in the
back.

Standing in March snow with Sister Rose Anthony

Five

Grade School – Again and Again

Annually during the 40s and 50s, on August 12th, the feast of St. Clare, all the sisters would gather in the college auditorium after supper. We waited for our name to be called to receive our "obedience," which was our assignment for the coming year. In silence, each sister would approach the Superior, take her envelope, then leave in silence to retire. It was a total secret as to where a sister would be next year. But the next day, all was shared.

One never returned to the previous convent to pack, so in June, at the end of the teaching year, everything a sister owned would be placed in her black trunk. If the sister did not return to the same convent, the superior would simply ship it to the new parish or school.

I was assigned to St. Jude's in Cleveland, Ohio, along with three other sisters. It was a new school in Warrenville Heights. Sister Rose Anthony was to be my guide on the train. She was young, but she had taught for seven years. We boarded the train at midnight at Union Station in Chicago. Sister Rose Anthony had a map, and I couldn't believe how far east Cleveland looked. The journey lasted ten hours. Every time I woke up we were still in Indiana.

We were exhausted upon arrival at the small white farmhouse we would call home. The Superior had been moved from a large, ethnic parish and school that she had been a part of for years. Looking back, her adjustment was probably bigger than ours. Here she was with three Irishwomen – Connor, Kelly, and Keating – and out in the country at that.

The yellow brick school became the center of my existence. I looked through the readers and arithmetic books for my second

Tom Sheridan

Sacred Heart students
Someone accomplished quite a feat in getting all of
my students to sign one card without my knowledge

graders and energetically decorated the bulletin boards, which I loved as it was my only creative outlet. I was to prepare the second graders for First Confession and First Holy Communion. I was lucky because my second grade class had been taught by Sister Ita, so they all could read.

My biggest revelation during my first year teaching on "mission" was that I was to be anonymous. My new superior, who was kind and good, reminded us that we were not supposed to tell students anything about ourselves, including where we were born. This seemed strange to me, and when faced with the question, "What state were you born in?" I simply replied, "The state of original sin."

One day a threatening snowstorm forced our school to close. We were to call our students' parents and say, "This is a Sister of St. Francis. Our school will be closed tomorrow due to snow." I was a little uncomfortable not saying, "This is Sister Martha, Jim's teacher from St. Jude's," but I chalked it up as another new lesson.

Grade School Again and Again

The most difficult event of my anonymity occurred during The Divine Office that we said at 4:30 p.m. A doorbell rang and I, being the youngest, answered the door. A young woman, 17 or 18 years old, asked if she could speak with Sister Martha. I told her I would be right back.

I told the Superior what the girl's request was and she said, "Tell her that she wants to speak to me." I was flabbergasted, but did as I was asked. I went back to the girl and said, "You do not want to see me; you want to speak to my superior." She looked at me dumbfounded. I returned to the chapel. I thought of my mom's stories, about nun saints. She'd say "If a Superior asked you to plant cabbages upside down, you must do it." I did it. Needless to say, the girl who had been directed by Father Eric to see me about entering the convent never came back.

Our convent had three small bedrooms and a bath upstairs, and a bedroom and bath on the main floor. Being the youngest, I was to share the downstairs bathroom with Sister Ita, whose room was next to the kitchen. Early in the year, I caught a bad cold and my superior told me to make hot lemonade and add some whiskey. I dutifully did this while I waited for Sister Ita to complete her bath – the cold lasted until the spring!

Franciscan priests operated the parish. Each afternoon, the assistant priest would come through the school to make sure the building was secure. He was a quiet, serious man who would stand in the door in his Franciscan robe and chat awhile. I wouldn't call it conversation because I was reluctant to say much. I never walked over to him to converse. Even that worried me because of the novitiate warnings about talking to priests and janitors. The pastor was a good man but was a bit old and crabby, and there were just the two priests in the parish. Looking back I realize how lonely the assistant probably was. I have mixed emotions, but knowing my propensity for taking care of people, it was probably better that I remembered my training and stayed at a distance.

Spring came and my class received their Holy Communion. As the children participated in the ceremony, I felt proud. This was what my life was about – preparing students to be good, devout Catholics. After the ceremony, I had to decline getting my picture taken with a communicant because it was against the rules. One parent had a movie camera and photographed me walking across the yard to the convent despite my plea.

Being with my class and preparing them for Holy Communion reminded me of my own Communion day at St. Patrick's Church in Joliet in May 1943. My class at St. Pat's was much larger, with 58 students, and Sister John Catherine, Order of Dominicans, prepared us diligently. My godfather, Uncle Tom, gave me white gloves.

While I was at St. Jude's, my brother Charlie took his bar exams, and I prayed for him with the second graders. One day as my class lined up in the school hall, I cautioned them to enter the room quietly. One clever boy, Patrick, continued to talk. I had him wait until last. Just as I was about to scold him, he looked up and asked me in a lisp, "Sister Martha, how's your brother Charlie?" Patrick reminded me of Ed Hennessy from my grade school class of 1949, who always had the perfect remark. There was also a pair of girls, a blonde and a brunette in my second grade, who reminded me of Kay Mannell and Joan White, other '49 classmates, who always had the correct answers and neatest papers.

Teaching is a science and an art, and each year I learned something valuable. But I think by the end of year one, I had learned fifty percent of what I'd ever learn. I also learned that second graders had personalities. One day the principal, who was also my superior, said, "Take the babies to the other end of the playground." I was insulted. "My second graders are not babies," I told myself. But, of course, I said nothing.

My formula for being a good teacher is to know the material and believe that it will enrich the students. The art and skill of bringing the two together is based on an appreciation of each student and the ability to discipline. I always encouraged students to listen to each other and to the teacher. Depending on the year and the class, I alternated between considering myself a good disciplinarian, and a poor one. Teaching is a skill learned by doing.

My first year, I learned much about teaching and convent life. Returning to Joliet was fun, and my classmates and I exchanged numerous stories.

My second year, I taught at St. Mary's in Des Plaines, a suburb *Grade School* west of Chicago. It was a school with sixteen classrooms, two for *Again* each grade. There were six young sisters assigned to this school. One *and* was my good pal and classmate Sister Mary Jean, who had been *Again* there the previous year so she could mentor me! As far as the convent itself, it was much easier because there was an established mode of operation, so I no longer had to cook and drive.

Teaching was a bit more difficult first semester. I taught 60 third-grade students in a corner of the school hall which had moveable walls. Each Wednesday, the walls were collapsed for bingo. This meant that my classroom had desks piled on each other and everything was pushed into a small space. Second semester, the principal separated the two third grades into a boys' classroom and a girls' classroom. I had seventy girls in a bungalow the parish had purchased. We had 69 desks, so one student was the traveler with her books in a box. There was always at least one student absent.

After lunch I loved leading the children in action songs. "When I was a lady... an actress... a nurse..." We would pantomime each career and sing loudly. I used the alcoves for reading groups. I liked being in charge of the whole building because it reminded me of my mom who taught in one-room country schools. I felt like I was both principal and teacher.

At St. Mary's as one of the youngest six sisters, my bedroom was a single room on the second floor. One evening after a feast day, we went upstairs to go to bed. One sister brought up a bottle of wine, which was left from dinner. We grabbed our cups and poured it around. This was during "great silence," the hours each night when we were to prepare for our morning meditation.

At the sound of our superior who had heard the talking, everyone disappeared into their rooms, and I stood in the long hallway holding the wine bottle. When I saw sister, I knelt to wait for my penance. Sister was so sweet and she almost apologized for giving me a penance or punishment for talking out loud in the dormitory area.

My co-conspirators said they heard me repeat, "That's ok sister – that's ok." I got lots of teasing the next morning.

My black trunk was next sent to Sacred Heart Englewood, a large parish on 71st and May Street on the south side of Chicago. There was a high school there and two classes of each grade. My superior was my senior English teacher, Sister De Sales. The neighborhood was great. The brick homes were close to each other and there were many Catholic families on the same block. I got to see my students racing their bikes and delivering our newspapers.

I taught three years at Sacred Heart – wonderful classes – one of them above

I taught sixth grade, which was fun. I had a few boys who had been held back more than once and were tall and starting to grow beards. Greek and Roman history was part of the curriculum and we'd have a history dress-up day.

We also had a fun religion class with Father Heidekamp who came each week to teach. I've always enjoyed drawing faces, and I taught my class my drawing tricks. One Friday we all drew pictures of Father Heidekamp. The collection of drawings was great, and Father Heidekamp and the other priests enjoyed the artwork.

48

On Sunday, the children went to 8:30 mass. Afterwards, four or five of my sixth graders came to my classroom to help correct spelling tests and arithmetic papers. I enjoyed having help, listening to them talk and laughing with them. That was more fun than being quiet at the convent as Sunday mornings were used for extra reading of spiritual classics.

After supper, in the nice weather, Sister Lauren, Sister Francis de Sales, and I would walk around the large block. This was the first convent that was in the middle of a nice neighborhood. I enjoyed the freedom of an evening walk with friends.

My next summer would be special because I would receive my gold ring of final profession. We made a ten-day solemn retreat. It was emotional because at the end of the retreat, we would make our final vows. This meant I would be a nun forever. It was a bit like having tenure, and I was so happy. I was almost dancing, and I felt embraced by the community. A tall young Franciscan led the retreat. He made us feel good about ourselves and our religious vocation. His talks were motivational. At one time during the retreat, I drew his picture and wrote a thank you note to him. I put it on his desk. I told him how much I enjoyed the retreat and to "keep up the good work." Next thing I knew, I was in the Mother Superior's office. Father had handed the note over to her as was the rule. She had to make sure that there was nothing romantic about my intentions. I admitted writing the letter and told her I had thought that it was very sincere and innocent. Nothing came of this but Mother Superior made it very clear to me that this was not allowed. I remember thinking there were so many things I couldn't do.

During the profession I placed my hand on the Bible and said, "Forever." As I later struggled in my decision to leave the convent, this moment was always in my mind and heart. My dad had always said, "Honey, if you are not happy, please come home." After that ceremony, he never asked anymore.

We wore a new habit and veil for the occasion. I was still not a seamstress and my friend Sister Euphemia did all the hemming and pressing, then gave it to me wrapped in a gift box for my trip to Joliet. Sacred Heart in Englewood was the first school to which I returned, and I felt like I was going home. When Charlie drove me there after my first summer at the Motherhouse in Joliet, the kids ran to the car to welcome me back. I was there for three years.

I had an idea in religion class one day. My classroom was adjoined to the principal's office, Sister De Sales'. There was a direct

Sixth Graders
giving me
Christmas gifts

Sacred Heart
School
1958 to 1961

Terry and Nancy Holz, brother
and sister, kept in touch with me

entrance into our sixth grade class, and one day I said, "If the Lord were sitting in Sister De Sales' desk, and we could each go in there one at a time, what would you ask the Lord?"

That night I read through the papers of the children's sincere requests: "Help my Grandma get better;" "New bike;" "Find my lost dog." But one paper stood out: "If the Lord was sitting there, I would be silent and just sit and look at Him." I was amazed and thought, "Mike is a natural contemplative" – Thomas Merton in my midst.

Later while I was working in Joliet, and my brother was Chief Judge of Will County, he had a case with a Chicago lawyer named Mike Fricaro who was representing a gambling operation. I quickly asked if he was short, husky, and smart, and Charlie said yes.

Grade School Again and Again

I was in the courthouse when Mike arrived. I asked him if he had attended Sacred Heart Englewood and then introduced myself. He was the one, but he didn't remember me. I was so disappointed. I did tell him the story, but I think it only embarrassed him.

Jesus meek and humble of heart Make my heart like unto Thine

Tom and Jim Sheridan

My three years of teaching sixth grade and being in charge of altar boys at Sacred Heart remain a special memory. It was a neighborhood that was just beginning to integrate. A sad memory is that many of the dear parishioners prayed hard to keep it white.

This was the end of my five years of teaching grade school: second grade at St. Jude's in Cleveland, Ohio; third grade at St. Mary's in Des Plaines, Illinois; and three years of sixth grade at Sacred Heart in Chicago. I did not realize that when I left Sacred Heart, it was the end of my grade school teaching career.

St. Patrick's Class of '49

Me

JMJD
Jesus,
Mary,
Joseph,
Dominic

Jim Biggins flew me from Sarasota, Fla. to Jacksonville, Fla. to see our 8th grade teacher, Sr. Rose Michael, O.P.... ....in his plane.

Grade School
Again
and
Again

More recently, Jim drove his motorcycle to visit Jack & me

Jim and I share July 29, 1935 as our birthday

Six

From De Sales to SFA

I have taught in prison for 12 years, grade school for five years, college for 15 years, plus short stints as an educator in an addiction unit facility and a Spanish center. However, my main expertise is as a high school English and religion teacher

Catholic schools grew rapidly in the 50s and 60s. That is why after only three years of college, we nuns went off to teach. After five years of teaching grade school, in 1961, I graduated with my bachelor's degree. I was assigned immediately to St. Francis de Sales High School on the East Side of Chicago near Lake Michigan and Indiana.

The school and convent were new and modern. The large white high school consumed the length of a city block. The convent was on the opposite side of the block and was connected to the school by a long portico. It was a spacious convent with many sisters; we had eight or nine grade-school teachers, 15 high school teachers, and two sisters who cooked for the 24 of us.

My first year teaching high school English and religion was as exciting and memorable as my first year teaching at St. Jude's. I was to teach junior and senior English classes and a freshman religion course. The textbooks arrived late, so my first day of teaching was based on my general knowledge. I was alarmed because I felt like I taught everything I knew on day one.

Adding to my feeling of deficiency, the other senior English teacher was Sister Mercia, a fantastic teacher who could recite ten soliloquies of Shakespeare. Sister had been my English teacher in high school, and I was in awe of her. Another Sister, Sister Laura, reminded me to be myself and not compare myself to Sister Mercia.

Class participation is a teacher's joy. In my junior English class I taught American Literature. They were a smart class. When we studied *The Miracle Worker* about Helen Keller I questioned, "Isn't it marvelous that to think we must have words? That is why vocabulary study is so essential – the more words, the more tools for thinking." The class questioned me and one young basketball player said I was dead wrong. So we planned a debate for the next week. It was a wonderful, heated debate! I don't think that there was a clear winner, but if there was it was the basketball player. Classes like that make me realize why I became a teacher.

The first year at St. Francis de Sales another group of juniors asked me to be their debate moderator. They assured me that they would do all the preparations and I only had to show up, and I said yes. So my principal and I went to a meeting where we were given the topics and the school we were to debate. It was the University of Chicago Lab School. We prepared and drove to Hyde Park for the event.

The opposing team appeared to be quite young and small. Perhaps they were gifted students and had been accelerated. A member of my debate team remarked, "They must have teethed on algebra books." We won by default because one of the lab school debaters lost his temper, but I don't think that we did that well. One of our team members looked blue and discouraged. Another teammate, Kathy, said to me, "Leave him alone – he needs a girl."

St. Francis de Sales was large and modern, and I enjoyed my classes. It was the 60s and the school masses were in the gym – with songs in English and students carrying up the bread and wine at the offering of the mass. To see the active participation of the students felt so encouraging to me.

In the same gym we had student dances over the weekend with Chicago DJs. I remember the first time I saw the Twist and heard it explained as "taking a large towel behind your back and drying your butt." We sisters tried it back at the convent.

I was startled one day when one of the sisters was taken to the hospital in the morning in an ambulance. What surprised me was that the sister was present at supper that same night, and there was no talk or explanation. When my mom landed in the hospital we were always so worried. My aunts would all call and come over. My dad, brother, and I rushed to her bedside. This incident with the sister seemed so cold. Why was no one worried? Years later I decided that she must have passed out from alcohol. Why else would it have been so quiet and so ignored? I never really knew.

During my year at De Sales, I watched as the 20-story Skyway to Indiana was being built. It was an engineering feat. In the morning I watched the sun come up over this "road in the sky," and in the evening it was the backdrop for the setting sun. Whenever I'm on the Skyway, I think of De Sales.

Over holidays or weekends we often rented reel to reel movies, which I loved. At Christmas we watched *The King and I*, and I found Yul Brynner very appealing. So I'd wink at some of the younger sisters and say, "Happy Yule-tide."

Happy "Yule" Tide! wink wink

When I packed my trunk in June of 1962, I didn't realize that I would unpack it twelve blocks away, still on the south side at 91st and Exchange at St. Peter and Paul's.

On August 14th, 1962, I arrived at S.S. Peter and Paul convent, grade-school and high school. Sister Anthony Marie, an older sister of Sister Mercedes who was my classmate, always called it the "little school with the big spirit". It was in the middle of the south side of Chicago at 91st and Exchange near Goldblatts department store.

"East side," or Saint Francis de Sales, had a new and modern convent. S.S. Peter and Paul's convent consisted of two old dark brick apartments with bars on the lower windows for safety. They were three story buildings. My room was on the lower floor of the second building and was quite isolated. It was like sharing a whole apartment with one other sister. There was a large front room, dining room and a small empty kitchen. There was a second bedroom occupied by Sister Jonathan. I used the dining room table for my books and papers – keeping all my things in one room was never easy for me.

Looking over my personal journal for my first year at S.S. Peter and Paul, 1961 to 1962, makes me both surprised and sad. I do record big things like the Cuban Crisis, the opening of the Ecumenical Council, and later the arrival of The Beatles.

I also realize how often I was sad. This was the first time I wrote in my journal, "I might need professional help." My first weeks there I was always excited when some of my former students from Saint Francis de Sales stopped to visit, since I was only 12 city blocks away. I think it was the first time I was truly homesick for my last school. Emily Mannarilli came to see me twice, and Judie H. sent me a sympathy card when poet e. e. cummings died.

One afternoon, Sister Celene, my superior, called me into her office. She had a photo of me in her hand that had been sent to her by the superior at Saint Francis de Sales. In the photo, I was wading in a small stream, with my long brown habit pulled up around my knees. I immediately recognized the occasion and the photographer. The librarian, a former religious brother, had taken it at a closing staff picnic in June. I was embarrassed seeing my legs, and that the photo was taken by a man!

The librarian had always been friendly. I thought that he recommended books to all the English teachers. I never felt that there was anything suspicious or inappropriate. I'm not sure there was, but having the photo sent to my superior scared me.

Sister Celene was very sweet as I tried to explain the photo. Sister then looked at me calmly and asked, "Are you hankering for a man?" I told her that I didn't think so. How right she was – but I didn't realize it.

These were hard years for my family back in Joliet. On September 16th, 1962, I jotted in my journal:

> *Mom – about the same.*
> *Dad – thinking he might have to sell the house.*

Prom Time –
Pat, Bernie,
Bea, and Marilyn

Yearbook editor,
Maureen Miller

Dianne Young as a
freshman and a senior

Charlie – starting with a new law firm on Monday. He doesn't seem extra happy. He's the president of St. Pat's CCD.

Mom had been in a hospital and then a nursing home. We knew that she was not going to get better because her bad heart and strokes had been going on for years. I had cried my hot tears years before. Dad never did sell the house, but I'm sure it took all his savings to keep my mom at Pleasant Center, a lovely nursing home in Joliet. *From* Charlie had been working hard to be successful at law. Each move *De Sales* was better, but he hadn't yet hit his stride. I was proud that he was *to SFA* head of the religious program at our home parish.

Despite the loneliness of my first months at SSPP, it turned out to be a great place. Each school day I ate lunch early back at the convent, and then returned to school to supervise the students. Students brought their lunches and after eating danced to records. I had a daily record hop and got to know most of the students. We were a school of 250 girls. As usual, I taught English and religion.

Sister Jonathan and I taught senior religion, and we had a "my class" versus "her class" debate on proving the existence of God. My class said, "You can't prove it," and Sister Jonathan's said, "You can." My class won, because you can't prove it scientifically.

S.S. Peter & Paul

I made lifelong friends at SSPP. In my freshman English class an assignment was reading *Great Expectations*. A freshman named Sue Bruno didn't like to read, but talked as though she liked to fight. I asked her to help with church work after school. Sister Sue is still doing church work as a member of the staff at the University of Notre Dame in South Bend, Indiana.

The Lamp

Vol. 31, No. 8   SS. PETER AND PAUL, CHICAGO 60617   June 4, 1965

Me

I served as editor and advisor to the school newspaper, "The Lamp" while I was at S.S. Peter and Paul in Chicago.

Nice tights

During my second and third year I moderated *The Lamp*, the school newspaper. My first editor was Maureen Miller who was very creative, hardworking and worried about her mother. Her father had died and her mother was learning to drive and date again.

At this time I was going home almost every week as my mother who had been in a nursing home was not getting any better. Maureen, her friend Barb, and I rode the bus together after school on Fridays. I was heading for the train on the same bus that they took home. I now receive photos of her wonderful grandchildren.

The next year, writer Bernie Smierciak and photographer Pat Pokrewynski kept me laughing and filled with strawberry milk shakes from Gayety's famous ice cream parlor on Commercial Avenue. We went to a journalism meeting at Marquette University and Pat couldn't fall asleep because she couldn't watch the *Tonight Show*. When we meet-and-eat, the laughter still continues.

My first year at S.S. Peter and Paul was finished. Seeing all my classmates back in Joliet made my summer joyful, but it ended with the death of my Mom. In my journal I wrote:

August 10, 1963
St. Paul's Convent, Joliet

Yesterday morning at 6:45 am Mom went home to God. We hadn't stayed though we knew she was low, because the nursing home preferred not. Charlie was at the convent door when I came from mass. I knew Mom must be critical or at rest. I asked Charlie if Mom was bad and he said, "Yes, She's gone." Dad met me at home in tears. He felt bad that I hadn't tried to stay. I had a feeling – but it meant red tape – and the week had been long. I think I was the only one with a strong feeling Thursday night. It was the way God wanted it, we must believe. So many times I had felt I was seeing her take her last breath.

The wake was just last night. Coynes did a wonderful job. Mom looked beautiful in a powder blue dress. My class – 10 sisters came. Sister Carolyn came later. All of them but Sister Alfred Marie were able to see mom.

Mother Borromeo and Mother Immaculate came. The Retreatants were not allowed to come without special permission which quite a number got. Sister Elizabeth Marie and Sister Eugene to name two.

All in all, everything went fine – thinking of Mom in heaven is a relief.

Jesus, thank you
and Grant Mom
eternal rest

The same year on November 22, 1963, President Kennedy was assassinated in Dallas. Three of us were in the church attic, sweeping and arranging the church decorations that were stored there. A sister came to get us, and our entire convent, with the entire nation, sat transfixed in front of our black-and-white television. I have a feeling that we might not have even said our prayers together those days. It was similar to the World Trade Center event of 9/11.

Another thing I associate with S.S. Peter and Paul is having the restrictions lifted on bathing suits. We all had black swimming suits, but it was decided that although we only swam at private beaches and pools, a group of women in black suits would draw attention to anyone passing by or boating by.

Our long brown habits with white cords belting us in and long scapulars, like floating aprons, hid our shapes. I remember one sister who was particularly sweet and small came home from a day of shopping and modeled her bathing suit for us. She was so well-endowed and looked so great that I remember being speechless. This was the first of many changes.

Another memory from S.S. Peter and Paul was being kissed by our janitor. I was to have a freshman homeroom of 38. The desks were old and mismatched and had some initials carved on them. In mid-August, I asked Sister Celene if I could rent a sander and then re-varnish the desks. The janitor helped me occasionally, and one day he leaned over and kissed me on the cheek. I was shocked and embarrassed. Nothing was ever said between us, before or after. I told no one! I knew I had done nothing wrong, but I didn't want anyone to know. At times like this I could hear Sister Anacleta's admonition: "Beware of priests and janitors."

My three years at S.S. Peter and Paul turned out to be very special. The predominant ethnic groups were Polish and Mexican-American. When the students would bring a food specialty, I would eagerly eat it. Koláče still remind me of my years there.

Each summer we returned to 520 Plainfield Road – shortened to 520. The first summers back, I finished my B.A. Then I enrolled in a masters of theology program staffed by Franciscan priests with their doctorates from Rochester, New York, where they ran St. Bonaventure University. I loved it, particularly the "De Triplici Via" (The Three Ways) of St. Bonaventure. He theologized that the whole universe could be explained by the Trinity. I found some butcher paper the size of a dining room table and outlined the whole thing. I think I loved the fact that the truth could be outlined!

Dad came to my summer graduation from the Seraphic Institute, as the theology program was called. He arrived early as he loved graduations. The annual graduation from St. Francis Academy, my high school, each June was beautiful. The graduates would line up at the school at the corner of Wilcox and Taylor and walk single file silently to the Cathedral, three blocks away. I found out later that each year after I had graduated from high school, he would still come to watch. After lunch I was talking to a Franciscan priest who had been my teacher. I remember feeling somewhat embarrassed that Dad found me talking to a priest.

In the summer of 1965, our community celebrated its 100th anniversary of our founding. The sisters who were musicians and writers in our community wrote a musical called *The Bells of St. Francis*. Some of my students from Saints' Peter & Paul came to see me say a couple of lines of dialogue. Our founder, Mother Alfred Moes, was not yet fully celebrated by our congregation. The centennial musical was based on everyday happenings in the life of our Sisters. Our congregation's 100th birthday was very important to me.

Georgian Pifko, 2nd from left in the back row, was my student and sent me pictures of her family for many years.

By 1965 I had taught grade school for five years and high school for four. I was in Chicago for eight of these years with only my first year being in Ohio at St. Jude's. My trip to Cleveland had seemed an interminable journey back in 1956, but in 1965, it was different. My dad and brother drove me to St. Peter's in Mansfield, Ohio.

My first impression of St. Peter's Mansfield on August 18, 1965, was that the town was tiny and the school was huge.

Our sisters had staffed St. Peter's grade school and high school for close to a 100 years. One of my college professors always told horror stories of teaching high school there. Mansfield was a town of about 30,000 in the north-central part of Ohio, and we were the only Catholic parish in town.

The staff of the Key News at St. Pete's in Mansfield, IL

Mary Ann Leach, one of my students

St. Peter's Golden Jubilee Celebration (1965)
Notice the similarity between the group of us and
the Last Supper painting on the wall

The convent was located on the top floor of the school. The door to the convent was through a special entrance with an elevator. So when the doorbell rang, we had to get in the elevator, go down two floors, and meet the visitor.

St. Peter's, a beautiful new school and convent, was more than twice the size of Saints' Peter & Paul. It was co-ed and had a winning basketball team and an excellent summer community theatre held in our auditorium. My first summer, I remember watching *My Fair Lady* from the balcony with two other sisters.

At St. Peter's, I moderated the newspaper, *The Key News*. Our principal, Sister Romayne, told me not to worry about expenses when I asked about the budget. The journalism room was on the bottom floor, and because of its size, it was called "the key hole."

From De Sales to SFA

Bernice was on the staff of the Key News. We had matching smiles.

I jumped into organizing *The Key News*. I took my class to the printing shop, and the owner explained the process of letterpress printing. It was done using lead plates, so once it went to press, any correction was costly. The paper was generally four to six pages long. Soon we were printing eight pages. Finally, Sister Romayne had to set limits. I would spend Saturdays working in the journalism room. It had a record player, so I worked while singing along with Mitch Miller. We had over 20 sisters and the years went quickly.

I taught two senior English classes, two junior English classes, and a Journalism class. I hadn't taught guys for three years and I was nervous. My first class was a class of seniors, and as I took roll call I knew I was in trouble. When I'd call a name they'd say, "He joined the Navy."

Ciscarama was an all Chicago Catholic schools presentation at McCormick Place in Chicago.

The students were talented

THE
CANTICLE
OF THE SUN

Most high, all powerful, all good Lord! All praise is yours, all glory, all honor, and all blessing. To you, alone, Most High, do they belong. No mortal lips are worthy to pronounce your name. Be praised, my Lord, through all your creatures, expecially through my lord Brother Sun, who brings the day; and you give light through him.

COME TO THE FAIR...

'64

TOP RIGHT. Spanish folk dancers Irene Bahr, Harriet Stacy (standing l. to r.) and Margaret Verduzco (center).

TOP LEFT. Japanese dancers (l. to r.) Mary Esther Cardenas, Margaret Campos, Mary Alice Pena and Anita Munoz.

BOTTOM LEFT. "Gigi" Yolando Palos.

BOTTOM RIGHT. Papa Joe's (l. to r.) Row one, Darlene Cotter, Ann Markovich, Marion Beaucaire. Row two, Lorrain Altamirano, Tina Ringo, Denise Pazuc. Row three, Karen Miller, Julie Ann Deveny.

CISCARAMA - MAY 7

Eventually this class got to be fun. However, my other senior class never did. I had to go through our large auditorium to get to that class. They were always one step from rioting when I arrived. I learned that if your class has discipline problems, always get to the classroom first to stake your territory.

One of my homeroom students tried to help me by writing me this note:

> Sister:
>
> You've helped me out so I think I'll tell you something. When I was a freshman I had Sister Stevens for Home Room. You know how neat she is. Anyway, she let us have our own way all the time and she never got anything done in her (spare) time.
>
> (THAT SOUNDS FAMILIAR DOESN'T IT?) You've been having trouble in home room and in English – THIS MY [may] SOUND ODD AND CORNY BUT – what you need to do is be a little more strict. I DON'T NECESSARILY [mean] BE AN OLD CRAB!
>
> Terry

Later when I gave an essay assignment, I learned that this same student was irritated with me. Here is the assignment.

Believing that the substance of writing does not lie so much in the subject as it does in the writer's attitude – his sensitivity, his perception, even his wisdom, students were asked to make vivid through a clear, concrete writing, a recollection of a person, place, or thing that was important to them. Examples were a classmate I'll never forget, a singer that started a trend, and a trip that changed my life.

This is the essay he wrote.

> It was the beginning of the school year and the days were hectic. Students ran from room to room, checking to see who their teachers were. My first stun took place when I walked into home room. There before me was a five foot, six inch nun who had a glow on her face that brightened the day. Her name was Sister Martha.
>
> At the beginning of the year, I had a large crop of hair that almost got me kicked out of school because it didn't meet the standards of the teachers. (Long, blond, curly hair that stretched over his shoulders) During

From De Sales to SFA

And he is beautiful and radiant in all his splendor! Of you, Most High, he bears the likeness. Be praised, my Lord, through Sister Moon and the stars; in the heavens you have made them, precious and beautiful Be praised, My Lord, through Sister Water; she is very useful, and humble, and precious, and pure.

67

the coming weeks I had problems with the Principal and coaches. Lecture after lecture, insult after insult rolled through my ears. Finally I got the hair out of my eyes and tears of embarrassment replaced it. The person that I least expected to laugh, laughed me out of home room. Yes, it was Sister Martha, the nun that understood everybody's problems but mine.

Terry

I apologized.

Discipline was an ongoing challenge. I think I generally disciplined by being nice, keeping the students busy, and using my "Connor" stare. My two aunts were teachers and they taught me well; "Never a word where a look will do."

But that senior English class my first year at St. Peter's is memorable. One guy threw a pocket knife at a cork bulletin board. I didn't feel aimed at particularly. I think I sent him to the principal, although no one was hurt. Today that would mean a police report and suspension. Maybe it should have then, too!

Because of my long walk between classes the students always had an opportunity to write on the board before this class. I would erase it and begin. One day there was a big "69" on both the front and side boards. There was more laughter than usual so I suspected it must have a sexual connotation. After class I asked one kind boy what it meant. He was so embarrassed but finally got enough explanation out that I knew it was a sexual position.

I taught in Mansfield for only two years. One special memory is of convent murals. The artist, Sister De Padua Antl, was stationed there both years. Sister decorated our long plain halls for St. Francis Day, Christmas, and Easter. They were beautiful chalk drawings on large sheets of paper, and I helped her put them up by learning to roll small pieces of scotch tape into small balls. She would use these to affix her murals to our walls. They were wonderful.

A parishioner had donated a very large Mercury car to the convent for our use. We always felt un-Franciscan when driving it. One Saturday I drove three journalism students and myself to a one-day workshop at the University of Detroit. In the middle of a large boulevard near the university the car stalled. I'm not sure which one of us discovered that we were out of gas, but since we were near a gas station, there was no accident or big delay.

It was evening when we returned from Detroit. I dropped each student off at his or her home. I remember that Bill Hahn turned white when I missed a stop sign. The last student was a senior who was very bright and a sort of rebel without a cause. We sat in the car by his house discussing religion and politics. Suddenly, I realized it was late, and that this was not prudent. Although I was just a short block from the convent, I hurried home.

On the same floor as "the key hole," Sister Stephen taught home economics. She had a suite with a kitchen, dining room, and living room. The kitchen had the latest equipment, including the first microwave that I had ever seen. Sister taught me how to use it. I still remember the first time I watched bacon cook.

From De Sales to SFA

The Missionaries of the Sacred Heart had an institution in Shelby, Ohio only a half hour from us. We would help them on weekends give seventh and eighth grade retreats.

One Friday I was so tired, I did not know how I would be able to help there. We sat on a bank by a river and the students said the rosary – a devotion to the Blessed Mother. During those 15 minutes I could see the students really listening to the meditations between the decades of the rosary. I relaxed, got energy, and thought "How good God is."

These were the 60s, and my first year at Mansfield my head was totally covered with my coif and veil.

When I came back the next summer the habit changes had begun. I wore a modified small veil and the front of my hair showed. An editor from my first year who had joined the navy stopped by in August to see me. We were both perplexed – his Bob Dylan long hair was now a crew cut. I thought, "You have no hair," and I could see his large eyes were saying, "You have hair."

My two years at Mansfield were busy. I went to Columbus for my allergy doctor, visited an environmentally-correct farm called Malabar, where Humphrey Bogart and Lauren Bacall got married. The author of *When the Rains Came* owned it.

There were beautiful rolling hills south of Mansfield. Mansfield and Cleveland were such different cities. The summer between these two years at Mansfield I finished my thesis, "The History of Celibacy in the Catholic Church" and graduated with my M.A. in theology.

The summer of 1967, I began my studies in English at the University of Illinois in Champaign. I also left Mansfield and was assigned to St. Francis Academy in Joliet, Illinois. I had mixed feelings about leaving but was mostly happy as I loved the academy.

Be praised, my Lord, through our Sister Bodily Death, from whose embrace no living person can escape. Woe to those who die in mortal sin! Happy those she finds doing your most holy will. The second death can do no harm to them. Praise and bless my Lord, and give thanks, and serve him with great humility.

FRANCIS OF ASSISI
Canticle Of The Sun

My High School Proms

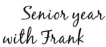

Junior year
with Jay

Senior year
with Frank

Sophomore year Style Show
for SDS: "Supply the demand
for the supply"

Seven

SFAges

I feel that Academy should be my middle name. I attended St. Francis Academy at Wilcox and Taylor from 1949 through 1953. Then as a young professed sister, I scrubbed the new Academy at Larkin and Ingalls to prepare for its opening in 1956. In 1967, I began my life as a teacher, which totaled seven years, until 1974. In 1978, I returned for eight additional years as co-principal, principal and president.

As did the old one, the new academy had a great reputation for academics. I was honored to be assigned there. I would be in Joliet, my dear hometown.

The one scary thing was that SFA was introducing "team-teaching." The plan was that each week there would be a one hour lecture on Monday for 90 students, and we would meet our assigned 30 students in groups of 15 twice a week. The idea was exciting, but I had never lectured for more than twenty minutes.

My teaching style had been more fluid, including lectures, oral reading by students, discussion, writing, and silent reading. So this was a new idea because I would no longer be "Queen of the Classroom." My team included Sister Gertrude Ann and Sister Donna, who were both excellent teachers, but my not being in charge required adjustment. Being on a team required humility.

As I walked the halls of the new Academy, I would smile, thinking of how much my high school years had meant to me.

It's hard to measure growth spurts in one's life, but my four high school years at the academy were seminal. Principal Sister Borromeo made sure that each teacher and student knew that we should focus on

*Lord,
make me an
instrument of
Your peace.
Where there
is hatred, let
me sow love;
where there is
injury, pardon;
where there is
doubt, faith;
where there is
despair, hope;
where there is
darkness, light;
where there is
sadness, joy.*

*O, Divine
Master, grant
that I may not
so much seek to
be consoled as
to console; to be
understood as
to understand;
to be loved as
to love. For it
is in the giving
that we receive.
It is in pardon-
ing that we are
pardoned. It is
in dying that we
are born again
to eternal life.*

ST. FRANCIS

*Memo:
from the desk of*

Mother M. Borromeo

Dear Sister Martha,

Thank you for your card from Grailville.
I imagine it did bring back memories
to you. Fifteen years is a long time.
I am glad you held to this intention you ex-
pressed that day -- "I hope to be
a Sister."

Now fifteen years later, may I add my
own hope to that first expression:
"I hope Sister Martha will always be the
cheerful, dedicated, apostolic Sister
that she is now."

And may she have a very happy year.

                    Devotedly,

                    Mother M Borromeo, O.S.F.

72

Christ. We annually had quiet three-day, all-school retreats with priests eager to inspire and direct us.

One priest said, "Decide what you are going to be and be it. Don't waste time. Be decisive. If it's not the right course, God will throw up a barricade, and you will be able to change course." I still agree with him.

Years before Petula Clark sang the hit, "Downtown," Cele, Rosie, and I had "Downtown" as our theme. Our day at SFA went from 8:30 a.m. to 2:30 p.m.. When our school day ended, the three of *SFAges* us headed for town, which was about three miles southeast of the Academy.

Three of our favorite haunts were the Louis Joliet Hotel, the Rialto, and the Joliet Library. All three were beautiful buildings. We talked and argued the entire way down Plainfield Road often discussing ideas inspired by our teachers. It was at this time that I was dubbed "Pope" due to my authoritative way of speaking.

Sister Elizabeth taught social studies to the sophomores. I remember her saying, "Don't criticize a Negro man for driving a new Cadillac while his home is sub-standard. He is not allowed to buy a home in a better area." She didn't emphasize the power of politics, but she got us thinking more clearly.

The Louis Joliet Hotel was grand with its heavy red carpets, chandeliers, and a fancy coffee shop where we could buy Coca-Cola and feel rich and grown up. Beautiful restaurants and hotels still have that effect on me. This hotel had more than six floors, so to us it was like a skyscraper.

A second magnificent structure was the Rialto Theatre, which covered a full block. The lobby faced Chicago Street and had doors on a side street and a back entrance on yet another. It was built in the 1920s for stage productions with a great organ that rose from the orchestra pit on a lift, while the organist played a triumphant march. The side and back entrances were not monitored. One day, I purchased a ticket and went to the side entrance to sneak Cele and Rosie in, but when I opened the first glass door to let them in, it closed behind me before I could open the second glass door.

Since my books were still inside the theatre, I had to go back. The film was *Zapata* with Marlon Brando. It was a great film, but we didn't care. We just wanted to sneak in. I just told the ticket agent that I had forgotten something inside.

We spent most of our time in a large, dark oak reference room, a side room of the library. The library was built of Joliet limestone and

Marge Connor ...
Peg O'Connell

*I played the lead in my
high school play:*
Peg O' My Heart

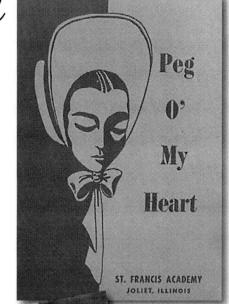

Peg
O'
My
Heart

ST. FRANCIS ACADEMY
JOLIET, ILLINOIS

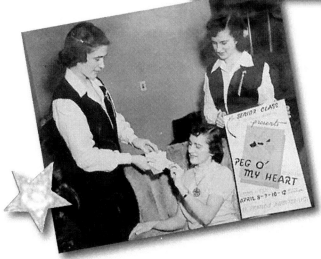

Peg O'Connell (Marge Connor) confronts the stern Mrs. Chichester (Rosemary Gudac). But love comes into Peg's life with Sir Jerry (Joan White) though Ethel (Cele Briick) protests "this romantic nonsense."

74

had a large stone sculpture of Louis Joliet in front. The city is named after Louis Joliet who traveled with Pere Marquette.

We did our homework together, but at exam time we did more. We made practice tests with blanks, and we even styled them according to the specific teacher. Looking back, I am amazed at our interest and industry. Between 4:30 p.m. and 5:00 p.m. we'd board our respective buses for home.

Rosie and Cele both had working moms, and my mother was sickly. I probably should have hurried home to help her, but she *SFAges* never complained. Cele was a tap dancer who became a wonderful poet. Rosemary was a natural politician who turned into a multi-talented artist. We felt like sisters. We each had a brother, but no blood sisters. We still see each other as often as possible.

At SFA I got my first experience of gathering with large groups of young Catholics. The Chicago Catholic high schools had regular quarterly meetings, and SFA would rent a bus and attend. Our teachers would join us. Being with them out of school felt special. I remember talking with Sister Albertus, our algebra and chemistry teacher. Her family was from Lockport, Illinois, as was the Connor side of my family. I loved these bus trips to Chicago with teachers and friends.

Some Sodality members signed up to go the Summer School of Catholic Action at a hotel in downtown Chicago. This was a gathering of high school students from the Midwest. Father Daniel Lord, S.J. (Society of Jesus) was a key speaker. He may have written the song "Soldiers of Christ." It was a triumphant anthem we'd sing at the end of large assemblies, and it was reminiscent of the Notre Dame fight song. I would get so fired up.

While at the academy, I learned how excited I was about all things Catholic and Christ-centered. I also learned that I had leadership skills. I was president of my sophomore class, vice prefect of the Sodality my junior year, and prefect my senior year. The Sodality was an all-school organization which focused on spiritual aims.

As sophomores, inspired by our English and Religion teacher, Sister Jean Paul, Cele and I hopped a Blue Bird bus to Chicago to hear and meet Dorothy Day, founder of the Catholic Worker Movement. I did not realize what a great honor that was. We also visited a Friendship House for the poor, founded by Peter Maurin, a friend of Dorothy Day. That summer I also visited Grailville, a community of Catholic lay women, in Loveland, Ohio.

My senior year was great. I was Peg of My Heart in our senior play, led assemblies as Prefect of the Sodality, and got the Bishop McNamara Award for Catholic Action.

My first year back at SFA as a teacher was not that exciting. My journal entry on October 20, 1967, says it well:

> *SFA – October 20, 1967*
> *Wow! It must be really bad when I make no entries my first months at a place.*
> *I wouldn't have believed how difficult it would be to adjust to team teaching.*
> *Sister Gertrude Ann, Sister Donna, and I are a team. We have 450 students – 11 seminar groups.*
> *My grades from Champaign: A in English; B in Journalism.*
> *Cele sneaked into a lecture – fun! Didn't see her 'til it was all over.*
> *1,000 strange faces – not being my own boss almost killed me.*
> *Right now I'm dead or I'd write some more.*

Many of my journal entries that first year focused on Charlie and Alice. Alice was divorced with three darling children: Tracy, 10; Darcy, 8; and Ted, 6. Alice ran the nursing home where Charlie took Aunt Kit for care. Alice looked like Debbie Reynolds.

Charlie started the proceedings with the diocese to get permission from Rome to marry Alice in the Church. Because Alice wasn't baptized, there was the possibility of the Petrine Privilege, a church law very seldom used.

> *March 22, 1968*
> *As much as I want to see him married, I look at it as a loss. My more intelligent self says that I'll gain a sister-in-law and nieces and a nephew.*
> *Lord help me accept Charlie as he is and myself as I am.*
> *Also help me to understand my vocation. Oh, I have to fight self pity.*

As the year finished, I wrote:

May 29, 1968

Today, with sweetness and sadness, I finished my last day of my first year at St. Francis.

I think if I were positive I was coming back, I'd feel a bit better. I guess I'd feel that the difficulty of adjusting was worth it. Maybe it was.

I talked to Alice yesterday and today. Yesterday she brought blue culottes by. Today I talked to her on the phone. She was rather depressed by the long chancery proceedings – and few answers. She doesn't want to become a Catholic yet and she sort of feels pressured.

I'm in my room – must force myself to correct exams.

Camelot tomorrow.

When I was a student at SFA, from 1949 to 1953, we had blue, soft-covered yearbooks called *Photo-Gems*. It was quite simple, but it had everyone's picture in it. I thought it was great. When I returned to the Academy in 1967, I learned that the yearbook had been dropped. I was very disappointed, and during my second year I had an idea. The Academy was to celebrate 100 years of existence, from 1869 to 1969. A history teacher, Ed Russell, and I approached Sister Jane Marie and requested a Centennial Book to celebrate SFA's unique history. We were only asking for a book for one year, and we got it.

I love books, history, and projects. We read all the old yearbooks with help from the community archivist, Sister Marian Voelker, and interviewed some elderly alumnae.

The project built energy. We found pictures of sports teams from the 1920s and matched them with current teams. There was so much help. There was a large student staff, and help from the art teacher, Beverly Decman, the librarian, Sister Paula, and Sister Marie Grunloh (Sister Euphemia). Ed and I pushed forward, and the aspirants helped.

This was my second year teaching at SFA, and I had another new job, helping Sister Ann James with the Aspirants. This was the last year for our prep and aspirant program. Girls who wished to be sisters came to Joliet to go to high school and begin learning more about religious life. Thus the name "aspirants" was given to those girls hoping to be Joliet Franciscans.

Charlie and Family

circa 1974 Back: Tracy, Darcy, and Ted
Front: John, Charlie, Matt, and Alice

Leaving for Hawaii - Back: Charlie and Alice holding Matt. Front: Darcy, Tracy, Ted, and John

In my religious class of 20 postulants in 1953, 15 of us had been aspirants. The program had a rich history, but the congregation realized that the concept no longer worked. The last year there were still eight aspirants, and they also helped with the centennial book.

Sister Ann James, the aspirants, and I lived in a new wing at SFA and operated as our own community. In the morning we would go to mass with all the Academy sisters in our beautiful chapel. In the evening we would pray together in our group of nine.

Sister Verene had been the previous director and the girls missed her. They also had a hurt attitude towards the congregation for closing the program. It was difficult to be the last students in a one-hundred-year-old tradition, but I enjoyed working with Sister Ann James and the Aspirants nonetheless.

Early in the year, Sister Ann James arranged for us to stay at a cabin on a Wisconsin lake. There were boats, and the girls were as anxious to row as I was nervous about a possible drowning. I insisted that they wear life jackets. Some were reluctant, so I walked towards the dock shouting, "Safety first!" and tripped over a rope. My laugh broke the brief silence, then everyone laughed.

Alice and Charlie

Charlie and Alice got married in the spring of this year. I was so excited to have a sister-in-law and two nieces and a nephew. Tracy, "T" for Theatre already knew she wanted to be an actress. Darcy, "D" for doctor, was talking about becoming one. Ted , "T" for tort, is a lawyer today. However, at that time, he wanted to be a pilot.

O God, be gracious and bless us and let your face shed its light upon us. So will your ways be known upon earth and all nations learn your saving help.
Let the peoples praise you, O God; let all the peoples praise you. Let nations be glad and exult for you rule the world with justice. With fairness you rule the peoples.
You guide the nations on earth.
Let the peoples praise you, O God; let all the peoples praise you.
The earth has yielded its fruit for God, our God, has blessed us. May God still give us his blessing till the ends of the earth revere him.

PSALM 67

79

Richard and Darcy's Children

Alec, Connor, and Rocky
about 1995

Connor, Rocky, and Alec about 10 years later.
Their joy in life continues

I loved being an aunt. That very first summer I took all three kids in their family station wagon to a farm in Kansas City, Missouri, to see my high school friend Sally Carey-Cutting and her husband's family. Tracy later talked about "this tall Aunt Muggs swooping down on them with a black veil."

Aunt Ruth and Muggs Boyd
at Charlie and Alice's wedding

Charlie was forty when he tied the knot. I had prayed for just this, year after year. Surprisingly, I felt displaced, a bit lonely, and jealous at the time. I loved being part of this wonderful new family, but Dad and I had moved to numbers five and six on Charlie's list.

Each year at the Academy got busier. I was always on a teaching team, first with Sister Gertrude Ann and Sister Donna, and later with Carol Prisbe and Ed Lagger. Ed was a brilliant reference on authors' lives, the opera, and Joliet history. Charlie thought that Ed's grandfather, who was a lawyer and mayor, was a hero. With dogged determination he fought the Joliet diocese for selling Saint Patrick's Field at the corner of Wilcox and Jefferson. It was supposed to have been kept for church use. He lost, but not for lack of trying.

There was a seminar group of 15 senior students who challenged me. We were discussing world literature: French, Spanish, German, and Latin. Many of the students were in their fourth year in these languages and had translated parts of this very literature. I was intimidated yet grateful; I think that I learned more than they did.

IT WAS IMMEDIATELY
CLEAR THAT YOUR
ABSENCE FROM OUR
KAFKA DISCUSSIONS
WAS NOT MERE
ILLNESS.

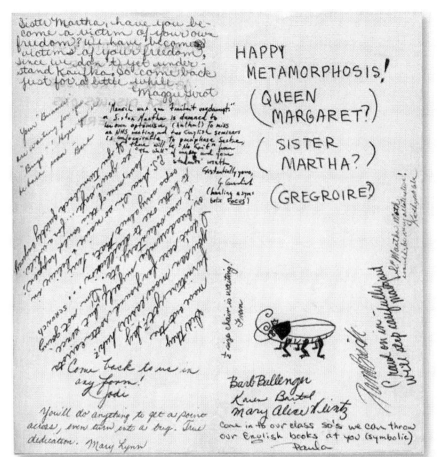

SFAges

While discussing Kafka's *Metamorphosis,* where the hero turns into a bug, I got sick and missed class. I still have the card the students sent accusing me of trying too hard to make my point. They even teased me that they had a tiny chair waiting.

One group of students that included my first cousin, Kay Borio, had me as English teacher for three straight years. It also included Pat Russell, Ed's sister, and Pat Gleason, one of the editors of the Centennial Book. They knew what I liked so well that they always ended up with A's.

It was in this seminar group of bright, loving girls that I realized how deep our prejudices are. I said that, "Even in our Catholic schools, the textbooks are lily white. There are no pictures or stories of black children." One of my favorite students took offense to my comment. She saw nothing wrong with that. I was shocked, even embarrassed.

Franscripts was a book with a softcover of the best student writing of the year. The English teachers would select essays, poetry, and stories from the entire student body to edit and publish. My third year at SFA, I was chair of the English department, and I became involved with the editors and moderators. The art staff would add

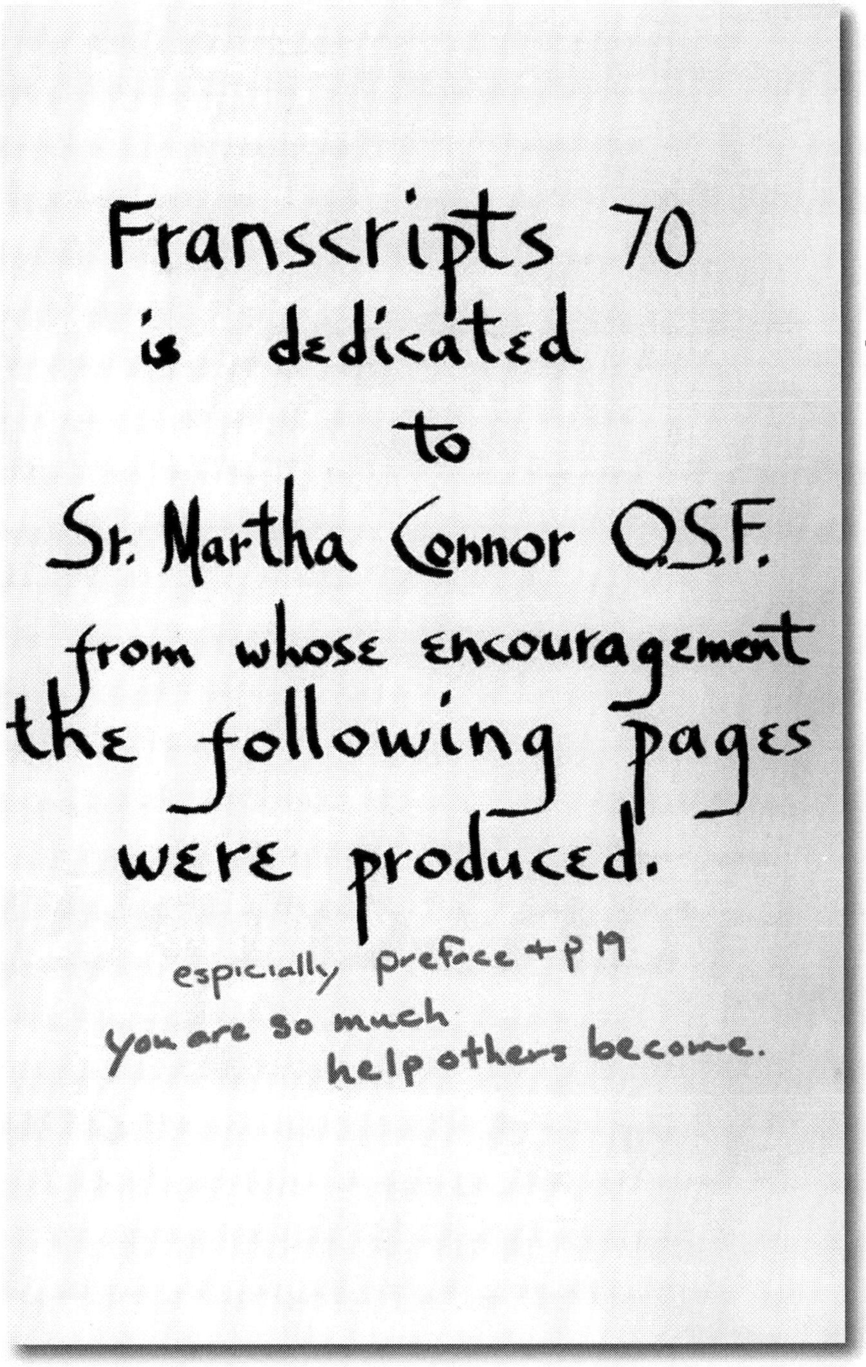

Franscripts 70
is dedicated
to
St. Martha Connor O.S.F.
from whose encouragement
the following pages
were produced.

espicially preface + p 19
you are so much
help others become.

visuals to the writing. *Franscripts* had been published since 1960, and I thought it was a great project.

When I opened the cover of the 1970 edition, I was shocked and pleased that it was dedicated to me. This may have been a ploy. For the next year I co-moderated it for the writing while Beverly

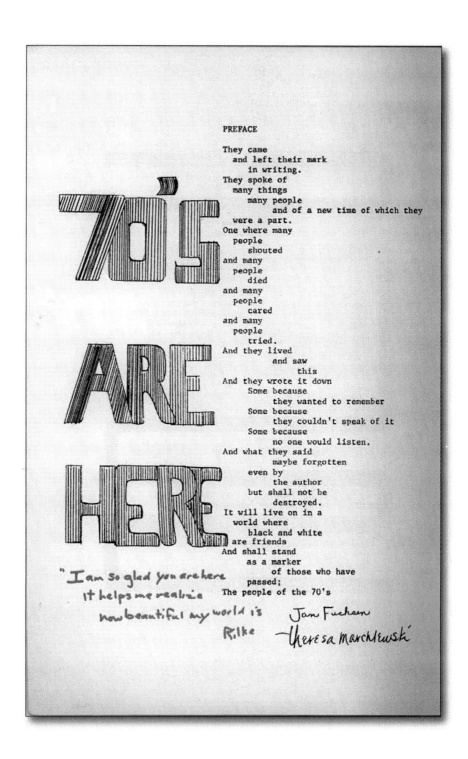

PREFACE

They came
    and left their mark
        in writing.
They spoke of
    many things
        many people
            and of a new time of which they
    were a part.
One where many
    people
        shouted
and many
    people
        died
and many
    people
        cared
and many
    people
        tried.
And they lived
            and saw
                this
And they wrote it down
    Some because
        they wanted to remember
    Some because
        they couldn't speak of it
    Some because
        no one would listen.
And what they said
        maybe forgotten
    even by
        the author
    but shall not be
        destroyed.
It will live on in a
    world where
        black and white
    are friends
And shall stand
    as a marker
        of those who have
    passed;
The people of the 70's

"I am so glad you are here
it helps me realize
how beautiful my world is   Jan Fuchen
            Rilke   —Theresa Marchlewski

Decman worked with the art department. The new dimension was that Bev selected artwork, and it was featured by itself.

After teaching English for three years, I began to teach religion. It was a mutual decision with Sister Jane Marie. My first team was Father Mark Fracaro, Jim Brady, and Sister Gerri Ronza. The seniors'

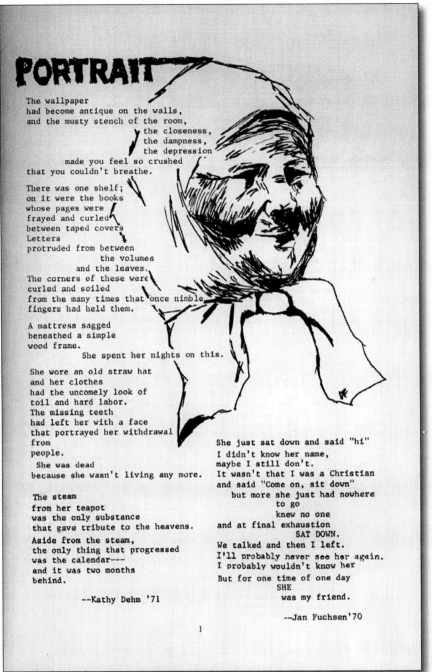

PORTRAIT

The wallpaper
had become antique on the walls,
and the musty stench of the room,
                    the closeness,
                    the dampness,
                    the depression
        made you feel so crushed
that you couldn't breathe.

There was one shelf;
on it were the books
whose pages were
frayed and curled
between taped covers
Letters
protruded from between
                the volumes
            and the leaves.
The corners of these were
curled and soiled
from the many times that once nimble
fingers had held them.

A mattress sagged
beneathed a simple
wood frame.
            She spent her nights on this.

She wore an old straw hat
and her clothes
had the uncomely look of
toil and hard labor.
The missing teeth
had left her with a face
that portrayed her withdrawal
from
people.
  She was dead
because she wasn't living any more.

The steam
from her teapot
was the only substance
that gave tribute to the heavens.

Aside from the steam,
the only thing that progressed
was the calendar---
and it was two months
behind.

    --Kathy Dehm '71

She just sat down and said "hi"
I didn't know her name,
maybe I still don't.
It wasn't that I was a Christian
and said "Come on, sit down"
        but more she just had nowhere
                    to go
                knew no one
and at final exhaustion
                SAT DOWN.
We talked and then I left.
I'll probably never see her again.
I probably wouldn't know her
But for one time of one day
                SHE
                was my friend.

        --Jan Fuchsen '70

SFAges

curriculum was World Religions. I remember Sister Gerri coming to class in a Chinese robe and the head gear of an eastern religion.

My next team was Father Mark and Mary Jo Burns. Mary Jo was interviewed during the summer when Father Mark, the chairman, was away. Mary Jo had taught one year in Chicago. I knew her slightly from her dramatic roles at Lewis University while she was at the College of St. Francis. Her résumé was impressive though the theology courses were basic. When I asked her if she was a practicing Catholic, she replied, "Yes." I said, "Fine, you're hired." She eventually earned a masters in theology at Loyola University.

A span of just 11 days during early 1970 was filled with life-changing events of loss and joy. Dad died, Aunt Rose died, and my nephew John was born.

Dad had gone to St. Joe's hospital for tests in July of 1969. This led to a gallbladder surgery from which he never fully recovered. He went back in the hospital December 24 and died January 23, 1970.

Charlie and I knew that Dad was failing. The doctor told us that his death was imminent. Hoping to give Dad an incentive to live, Charlie told him (before he told me or anyone else) that he was going to be a grandfather. He lived for eight more months.

I was so grateful for the private nurse that Dad had the days before he died. In the evening of the day he died, the nurse told me that Dad's breath was getting shallower. Before he took his last breath, the nurse removed some tubes. Dad truly looked at peace. Charlie and Alice were in Chicago, so I called them and then my cousins. I think Fran and Virginia were the first to arrive.

The McCauley Clan is always helpful.

The wake is a blur, but I remember coming to my bedroom at the Academy and finding a beautiful drawing of my Dad by Sister Karen Keitzman. The sisters were wonderful.

Then January 30, one week from the day Dad died, his name-sake, John, was born. It was a joyful day.

The day John was born, I was teaching a small group seminar. The principal, Sister Jane Marie, called over the loudspeaker, "Sister Martha, please come to the office." Charlie stood in the office beaming. He wouldn't tell Sister if it was a boy or a girl until I could listen.

Three days later, I had an early morning call from Charlie. Aunt Grace had died. I promptly drove two miles to her apartment. Aunt Rose, Aunt Grace, and Uncle Matt all remained single and stayed home to take care of their mother, my grandma. I was there before the undertaker took Aunt Grace's body from her bed.

Charlie and I, as we had done eleven days earlier, went to the funeral home to make arrangements.

That night I did something extremely brave, something one would do only out of love. I stayed overnight with Aunt Rose and slept in Aunt Grace's bed where I had seen her dead that morning.

Aunt Rose and Aunt Grace Connor were both teachers and both stayed at home with Grandma. They always slept in the same room in twin beds. I could not bear the thought that Aunt Rose would spend that first night alone.

What I had hoped would happen did. In the school year of 1971 to 1972, the yearbook was reinstated. For two years Bonnie Keenan from the theology staff moderated the book, and it was very philosophical and edgy. Ed Russell was the business manager.

As I said, I love books and projects and for the school year of 1973 *SFAges* to 1974, I was the moderator of the yearbook, *Catch*. I was living at St. Joe's convent in Rockdale and started staff meetings there in the summer. We decided to make the book format like a calendar and set all the pages horizontally, rather than vertically. Our publishing representative, Joe Feehan, who had helped us with the Centennial Book, checked with the company and gave us the go-ahead.

A group led by Sue Amberly, the editor, attended a workshop on yearbooks at Northern Illinois University. The theme they selected was: "The world doesn't stop while school goes on. There is always something happening both 'inside and outside.'" References to Nixon's scandal, Agnew's resignation as Vice-President, and Gerald Ford becoming the President were part of the monthly calendar.

Three student artists were spectacular: Claire Marozas, Julie Collins, and Mary Emich. And I, of course, had fun selecting pictures like the senior prom pictures of three of my cousins, Ruth O'Leary, Sally Boyd, and Debbie Havidich. When I look at this yearbook now, all the action in one year overwhelms me.

The seven years I taught English and religion at SFA were years of change. I remember planning an assembly on Betty Friedan, the author of the 1963 book, *The Feminine Mystique*, which made her the patron saint of feminists. I had not heard of her, but one of the National Honor Society members had and convinced me of her merit.

Each year at the Academy was busier and more fun. I received my masters in English from University of Illinois in Champaign in June 1972. The habit was simplified and some of the rules were relaxed. Sisters could join lay teachers and go out to a restaurant-bar after the prom or parent-teacher conferences, or stay up to watch Johnny Carson at night, as long as they made it to morning mass.

I was getting restless, so when Sister Lourdette suggested that I come to St. Procopius, where the students were Mexican-American, it sounded like a good idea. Without hesitation, I decided I would go.

Memories that last ...

High school teaching provokes memory

by Sr. Martha Connor

When I was taking Educational Psychology at the College of St. Francis from Sr. Dolores, she told me that she thought I'd be good working with primary grade children, but because of my height I would probably end up teaching high school. That's exactly what happened.

In 1961, St. Francis De Sales parish in Chicago had a brand new, very modern high school. It was at the easternmost part of the city, near the Indiana border. The faculty matched the edifice. It was my first year teaching high school, and our core book for literature was being delivered late. By the end of the first day, I was convinced that I had taught every bit of literature that I knew. It was a good thing that Sister Johanna Didier had advised me to just be myself in the classroom.

One of my parallel teachers was Sister Mercia Gillivan, who made Shakespeare come alive year after year. Sister Laura Filipas encouraged me daily.

I felt surrounded by great talent. Sister Magdalita Morvay was principal and superior. Sister Eileen Bannon (Rose Francis), Sister Therese Tusek (Stephen), and Sister Laurelle Berkes directed a spectacular 'Brigadoon'. Sister Lillian Zenz (Albert) moderated the newspaper.

In 1962, I was transferred to Saints Peter and Paul High School in South Chicago. Instead of the Skyway, I could see Goldblatt's and, just around the corner, Gayety's Sweet Shop. Sister Janet Rieden (Jonathan) moderated the newspaper and taught English and religion.

Sts. Peter and Paul had been nicknamed the 'little school with the big spirit'. It shared a corner building with the grade school and the church.

St. Peter's, Mansfield, Ohio, had a long and interesting history. For years it was the only Catholic church in the city and the only Catholic grade and high school. The Spartans were a championship basketball team. Sisters Laurelle, Eileen, and Therese Tusek directed and staged 'Sound of Music'.

The faculty lived on top of the high school. I was moderator of the 'Key News', the school newspaper.

In the spring of 1967, I received my ministry card, missioning me to St. Francis Academy, Joliet. I was returning to my Alma Mater. Sister Christine Fahrenbach (Hortense) was the principal, and the new school was only ten years old. I team taught English and literature with Sisters Gertrude Ann and Donna.

After three years in the English department, I started teaching theology, teaming with Father Mark Fracaro and Mary Jo Burns. For the first time, I taught the daughter of a former high school classmate, Maureen Andrews. For the first time, too, I was teaching with some of my own teachers, Sister Elizabeth Bertels and Sister Marie Grunloh, (Euphemia).

After teaching Christ and His Church to high school seniors, a course which stressed the need for the Church to be present in the inner city, I said 'yes' to Sister Mary Lucas (Lourdette) who had asked me to come to St. Procopius in Chicago. Situated in the Pilsen area, St. Procopius is 97% Hispanic. I started studying Spanish with Sisters Mary Ann Clarke and Cindi Meyer. I found sharing the Hispanic culture exciting.

My return to St. Francis Academy as co-principal with Larry Johnson was facilitated by Sister Lois Prebil. There were Sister Robertine Bluth and Jubilation, Franciscana, the Parent Board, Sister Anna Marie Becker and the alumnae.

What is rewarding about high school ministry? What makes high school an exciting place? In June, as I sat watching the Class of 1987 graduate from Holy Trinity High School at Division and Ashland in Chicago, I smiled at the thought that this was the 25th time I had done this as a member of a high school staff. I had been part of graduations at St. Francis De Sales; Sts. Peter and Paul; St. Peter, Mansfield; St. Francis Academy; and St. Procopius. I know that the joy and excitement that my high school ministry has given me have been generated to a great extent by the enrichment and vision of Mother Borromeo Mack and her Christ-centered curriculum during my student days at SFA.

No one could ever estimate the hours spent by those in high school ministry, hours spent with sodality, mission activity, plays, yearbook, funfares, raffles, retreat programs, youth conventions, and athletic rallies. No one can estimate the difference that a hope encouraged at this stage of life can lead to.

Sister Martha Connor teaches at Parkside Medical, an inner city substance abuse program for youth, located in Lincoln West Hospital.

Sr. Martha Connor talks with a student in her class at Trinity High School in Chicago. This student was a member of the 25th graduation witnessed by Sr. Martha.

At this point in our convent history, we could make suggestions about yearly placement. I believed that the church should concentrate on the Mexican population because it was growing and had a strong Catholic background.

I thought that working in an inner city would be good for my vocation because I was so at home in Joliet and my temptations were growing. I thought that this new work would make me focus more on my religious life, but this was not to be.

Jan Fuchsen,
Editor of
"Franscripts." She
became a nurse and a
missionary

Diane
Kreiger,
Student
Council
President,
now a
chiropractor

After 100 years, the prep school closed.
The last Prep Seniors at graduation
Nancy Scardina, Barb Schimpf,
Mary Jo Gruel, Janie Roper

DE COLORES

*De colores, de
colores se visten
los campos en la
primavera.
De colores, de
colores son los
pajaritos que vi-
enen de afuera.
De colores, de
colores es el arco
iris que vemos
lucir.
Y por eso los
grandes amores
de muchos colo-
res me gustan
a mi.
Y por eso los
grandes amores
de muchos colo-
res me gustan
a mi.*

*Colorful colorful
are the fields in
the springtime.
Colorful,
colorful are the
little birds that
come from far
away.
Colorful,
colorful is the
rainbow that we
see shining.
And that is why
I like wonderful
colorful things.
And that is why
I like wonderful
colorful things.*

View from the rooftop of
St. Procopius, Chicago

92

Eight

Pilsen and St. Procopius

Do good memories rise to the top when we reminisce? When I say "Pilsen," I think of a wonderful neighborhood: Quince Años; parades; "Las Mañanitas" early on December 12; Maggie leading "De Colores;" Suzanne planning the yearbook; and Vince and Zosia producing the plays. I think of Sister Mary Ann, Sister Cindy, and I taking Spanish classes at Loop College, Sister Josie and Sister Austin always listening and praying for us, and Linda and Dale falling in love. But when I reread my journal, it seemed bleak. I often speak of loneliness and adjustments.

When I volunteered to teach at St. Procopius High School in the Pilsen Area in Chicago, I had no idea how rich the cultural community was. The area of 18th and Racine in Chicago was an entry port of many Mexican families coming to the United States. The name Pilsen came from early immigrants of Bohemian and Czech descent.

As I look back, I was looking for a geographical cure. This is a term in 12-step programs, which means a new location will quell your demons. It doesn't work in 12-step programs, and it didn't work with me. But it was a distraction and a rich learning experience for me.

Two important mentors during these four years were Maggie Phair and Sister Lupita Cordero, SND. Maggie was a young woman who graduated from a Catholic college and had spent a year in Peru. She knew Spanish and was so enthusiastic about her first job teaching. She was determined to participate in the cultural dimension of the neighborhood. One of my first memories was marching with our

Jubilosos, jubilosos vivamos en gracia puesto que se puede. Saciaremos, saciaremos la sed ardorosa del Rey que no muere. Jubilosos, jubilosos llevemos a Cristo un alma y mil más, Difundiendo la luz que ilumina la gracia divina del gran ideal, Difundiendo la luz que ilumina la gracia divina del gran ideal.

Joyous, joyous may we live in the grace of He who wills it. May we quench the burning thirst of the King that does not die. Joyous, joyous we shall bring to Christ a harvest of souls, Spread the illumination of the divine grace from the great ideal, Spread the illumination of the divine grace from the great ideal.

93

students on 26th Street in a Mexican Independence Day Parade. I'm sure that our participation was something Maggie had arranged.

Maggie also arranged to have an artist-in-residence program Her fiancé, Ed, was a lawyer and did the paperwork to establish the Pro Arts Studies as a not-for-profit agency with Rita Bauman as the main visual artist. She had a space near the school.

Maggie also had a beautiful soprano voice and when the Parish Assistant, Benedictine Father Terence Fitzmaurice, heard her, he asked her to do the "Las Mananitas" on the feast of Our Lady of Guadalupe on December 12. That meant that Maggie would leave home by 4 a.m. to sing at the 5 a.m. mass and ceremony. The church would be filled with roses and participants. It's a beautiful experience. In Mexico it is a state holiday, and some factory owners have picnics for their staff and families.

Sister Lupita, the principal of the grade school, was Mexican-American and was dedicated to the church community in the larger Pilsen area. When representatives of the various Catholic churches met, it was a called a cluster. Sister Lupita was active in our cluster and I was delighted to go along.

Station Four of the first outdoor living stations at Pilsen 1973

This led to my being one of the team of organizers of the first Pilsen Living Way of the Cross productions. It was in 1977, and it still continues today. I was to assemble the fourth station, when Jesus meets his Mother. The girl playing Mary went to our high school but did not live in the neighborhood. The soldiers were teens that Father Terence was trying to keep out of gangs and out of jail. He was called out at all hours of the night for help. The youth were brothers of our students and we got to know them well.

One night after practice, I was to drive the girl playing Blessed Mother home. One of the boys had a driver's license permit, and I let him drive. Near the girl's home he spotted some young men he didn't want to see. He made a hurried right turn, and I thought he wasn't going to negotiate the turn correctly. I grabbed the wheel and we clipped three cars.

Pilsen
and
St. Procopius

The driver's main fear was that Father Terence would find out. By the time the police came, I was in the driver's seat. Father Terence never found out. I remember saying to the policeman, "I am in a strange neighborhood and bringing 'Blessed Mother' home from practice." I think I was driving a family car lent to me by Charlie. Surprisingly, there weren't any lawsuits.

I had another conversation with a police officer while at St. Procopius. It was an early Friday evening, and I had walked over to St. Ignatius High School on West Roosevelt, about six blocks away.

One of the Jesuit priests was my spiritual director and confessor. I started to walk back home, sauntering along with my purse dangling over my shoulder. I had to pass a large high-rise and walk through a dark viaduct about a block long which opened up at our school yard at 16th and Allport. There was traffic going both ways.

Suddenly a young, thin, black boy rode up to me on his bicycle. I thought, "I can handle this." Then he held a gun at me. I had no idea whether it was fake or real, but I immediately handed over my purse. I wanted to do something to alert traffic, but I couldn't be helped. No one noticed.

As I handed him the purse I pleaded, "May I please have my driver's license?" He declined and rode away. I followed him for a half of block, then walked home. As my keys were in the purse, I had to ring the bell at the convent and announce my plight.

A policeman came to interview me. After he finished he said, "I had nuns for grade school," and commented on their strictness. I said, "Don't complain, I bet you have good penmanship." He hesitated and then he said rather sheepishly, "Yeah, I do."

St. Procopius had a relaxed familial feeling. The entire school body totaled about 120 girls or less. Each year we had a Thanksgiving dinner that each class celebrated. The menu was planned and then students would volunteer to buy or make items. The students col-

St. Procopius Class of '75 (and me)

lected money for the class turkey. We'd divide the gym into quadrants, put up tables, and celebrate. The first year I was rather amazed when it all came together.

Our Lady of Guadalupe – Pray for us.

Another aspect of ease and freedom were student field trips. We had the Chicago bus system which held over one hundred people per bus. If a class of thirty went to the Chicago Stock Exchange or the Chicago Art Institute, we would just get permission slips and walk to the corner for the city bus.

We could plainly see the Sears Tower which was just sixteen blocks north of our school, and we were just twelve blocks from the University of Illinois, Chicago campus. We took advantage of our location. The admission counselors from University of Illinois, Chicago easily came to talk with the seniors.

96

I had the senior homeroom my first year, and I think that at least six of my students entered University of Illinois that year. I know that one became a doctor (Olga Nuño) and another one became a nurse (Alma Velazquez) who later worked back in the Pilsen neighborhood. It was an exciting school.

The staff of our school was young and ambitious. At 41, I was the oldest teacher. Our curriculum was approved by North Central Accreditations, but it was very basic. I taught English and religion. One time I taught Spanish, driver's education, and art.

Although 99% of the students were Mexican-American, there were differences I quickly learned. Many of our students were born in Chicago. If their parents were second generation, it was possible that they knew little Spanish. Students whose parents had come from Texas simply considered themselves American.

Pilsen and St. Procopius

Other students had just arrived from Mexico and felt homesick and displaced. They only knew Spanish and reluctantly learned English. They considered themselves Mexican only.

There was also a middle group who were happy that they were Mexican and American. Out of this group came the class leaders.

At the senior prom, they often requested two bands – one English-speaking and one Spanish-speaking. Generally, because of limited funds, there was a compromise

I also quickly learned about downtown Chicago. Being sixteen blocks from the Chicago loop made it handy for my Joliet friends to stop by and pick me up on the way into the city. I got a quick introduction to the restaurants and places of entertainment in downtown Chicago.

Tuesday, November 12, 1974
This past week has been hectic. Last Wednesday.
MJ Burns, MJ Davey, and Gerri Girot took me out
on the town for pizza and wine at Gino's on Superior
and then to Emerald Isle for genuine Irish Music –
Really fun – Home at 1 a.m.
Thursday – Dinner – Bonnie Keenan Staltzer &
Debbie Fumagalli – Berghoff's – Studied the Chagall
and 2 Calders. Home early 7 p.m.
Friday – Shopped with Maggie Phair for "Candy
Court" – home at 6:45 – then out with Sheila Bundy.
Went to Lawry's – tremendous dinner – then St.
Boniface – back by 11 p.m.

Saturday – Worked hard on charge and bed-
room (helped with CCD in a.m.) – then 7 – out with
Charlie & Pat King & Pat's brother Bill – Fire Place

Students from St. Procopius at celebration in 2000

Inn on Rush – then a walk through Old Town –
Then "Orphan's" – for a folksinger Barbara Dean –
Fun. Pat and Charlie not too keen on singer.
Sunday – worked in school – made a roast –
wrote letters
Monday – Candy Court – Kids to Mundelein –
Then Mark, his brother Bob (Chip) and a Ken were
waiting – off to Hanna East – a Japanese Restaurant
and a Fellini film.
Out five of six nights. At work, the next days look
hectic – but not socially!

The first question my students asked when I arrived was, "Have
you been to Mexico?" After my second year at St. Procopius, two of

my friends, Mary Jane and Deb, signed up for eight hours of Spanish in Mexico City. This summer study in Mexico trip was led by an architectural professor from Illinois State at Bloomington. I would be traveling with mostly college students, but I had three friends on the trip, Mary Jane, Deb, and a girl who was in my Spanish classes at Loop College. When we arrived at the awesome Mexico City airport, we felt like orphans. We were assigned groups according to our living quarters.

I always look for celebrities at airports. So when I saw a tall hand-some man at the Mexico City airport with charisma and a body-guard, I was sure that he was a movie star.

While I was staring at him, he started walking towards our particular small group. I was delighted when he said that he and the other gentleman were to chauffeur us to our summer home.

A beautiful young lady in our group who was from Connecticut, and fluent in Spanish, caught his eye. So the rest of the six weeks, he and his bodyguard kept close.

When Enŕique, the handsome gentleman, came to take Jody, the Connecticut girl, to soccer games or cultural events, I became her chaperon and thus became acquainted with the bodyguard, Antonio. Enrique had a bodyguard because he was a member of PRI, the reigning political party.

Antonio and I managed to converse haltingly with the aid of our English and Spanish dictionaries.

That summer, Enrique and Jody got engaged. I cautioned Jody to first tell her parents that she was dating someone before full disclosure. They had a fairy-tale wedding in October. I kept in touch with them for enough years to have pictures of their first three children.

In addition to our classes each day, many side trips were part of the experience. We visited Cuernavaca, San Miguel de Allende, and the pyramids at San Juan Teatihucon. During a short break, I visited Guadalajara where my student Olga Nuno picked me up and drove me to Ayutala, her home of origin. Her family was hospitable.

Another weekend, Debbie Fumagalli took us to the Polyforum Cultural Siqueiros which featured the March of Humanity showing the growth and interrelatedness of all people. It remains the greatest museum I have ever visited.

The only place in Mexico that I didn't enjoy was Xochimilco, a canal in the city famous for boat rides in decorated flat boats. It was completely commercial and the canal was not clean.

Living in the city, pushing my way onto a crowded bus each morning, and studying at UNAM was overwhelming.

My Spanish improved. When I came back, I could say "me gusta la gente," "me gusta la clima," "me gusta la comido," and "pero no me gusta estudiar."

Spending six weeks in Mexico, without being identified as a nun, taught me new things about myself.

I enjoyed the freedom of anonymity. It had been 23 years since I could just be myself. Enjoying this magnificent city, chaperoning Jody and Enrique, and sharing the experience with so many new people loosened a stone in my foundation as a nun.

My four years at Pilsen were rich. I still compare the Mexican restaurants I visit to the ones in Pilsen. Whenever I attend a new church, I am always thrilled to see an Our Lady of Guadalupe Shrine. And I still support the United Farm Workers started by Cesar Chavez.

The teachers at Procopious, like Maggie, Suzanne, Linda, Dale, Zosia, are still close. Dr. Olga Nuno and I remain lifelong friends.

On February 25, 1976, I wrote in my journal: "I didn't get one vote in the community election. Elizabeth is vice-president. Great."

In the next years, I was not elected as a voting member of our election year chapter. I remember being surprised.

When I was a younger sister, I had been elected to important committees. I wasn't sure why I had lost favor. My restlessness must have been clearer to the congregation than it was to me.

However, in the spring of my final year at St. Procopius, I was offered a great community job. It put my heart and brain in a new gear. I was asked to be principal of St. Francis Academy.

This last year Maggie, Zosia, and I were a team as Co-principals at St. Procopius. We pooled our talents and managed to do pretty well. Maggie, fluent in Spanish, did all parent functions. Zocia, with her business acumen, did the finances and correspondence. I did teacher evaluation and janitorial management.

I'm not clear as to how co-principal became part of the discussion for SFA, but I agreed with it. There was some discussion of Sister Lois Prebil and I as co-principal, but Lois wasn't sure that we had the same managerial and educational beliefs.

Larry Johnson, who had worked with our sisters in Lombard, was eventually chosen as the other co-principal.

I was extremely proud and happy but also scared and nervous about my new position at SFA. I left Pilsen, but my heart still warms at all things Mexican.

Nine

Co-Principals

I arrived back at SFA on the 25th anniversary of my own gradua-tion. This was to be my favorite job ever! The Academy had a couple of rough years and I was so anxious to put that behind.

The first time I stood in front of the Senior Class of 1979, I asked, "Who feels like a senior?" I don't think one hand went up.

I remember thinking everyone must feel green and nervous in a new title – senior, mom, principal, and widow. We grow slowly into new roles.

The previous June, the person who single-handedly took Larry and me "through the ropes" was Sister Lois Prebil. Lois had been acting principal for one semester and assistant principal for four or five years with Sister Alicia.

Sister Lois welcomed Larry and me, then gave us a carefully indexed notebook on all major topics, including "Jubilation," "Fran-ciscana," and "parent school board." We were so grateful for her mentorship, and we tried to thank her by making a collage of her days of service at the Academy. I think she knew how thankful we both were at her grace in passing on the keys.

While I was still at Procopius in Pilsen, I had started a summer program at Notre Dame which led to a Master of Science and Administration degree. I remember coming from Chicago to South Bend the summer before. My first thought when I stepped on the green pristine campus was, "This is a Catholic Disneyland." It was so different from Pilsen where I never saw a sunrise or a sunset.

Administration Team of '79: Mary Jo Moran, Sr. Robertine Bluth, Margaret DeSalvo, Larry Johnson, & me

Co-Principals

Mike Viollt (Chairman of the guidance department, now President of Robert Morris College) talks with a concerned parent

Robert Morris College

Co-principals

Theology Staff: Dan Roller, Sr. Lorraine Russell, Me, Sr. Kathryn Anderson, Larry Johnson, and Bob Cambic

Growing into New Roles

One of my favorite times of the year as co-principal – revving the students up with my 'welcome back' speech

But....my most memorable moments have been...
GRADUATIONS

Sr. Martha congratulates valedictorian Karen Christiansen '82.

From Seniors to Alumnae 1979

But the classes were well worth the journey. I had great professors and great classmates, many of whom were also religious sisters and brothers. My professor in Organization and Management became my guru. He was very perceptive, so I scheduled a conference with him and Larry so that we could have a smooth start as co-principals. It was a difficult concept and the professor acknowledged that.

My Notre Dame professor was very specific about our first faculty and staff meeting. He said to us, "If Larry speaks for five minutes, then Martha you speak the same amount." We were careful to arrange our agenda that way. He also cautioned us to support each other's decisions so that staff never had to go to both of us for an answer.

This was the same professor who had us read Peter Drucker's book, *Theories Of Management*. His central point was building on strengths, which led us to the motto of "Celebrate Our Strengths." We gave out t-shirts proclaiming our aim for the year.

The Academy had so many great things about its 100 plus years, and our greatest asset was the staff. We honored all the administrators, teachers, and staff who had served SFA for ten years or more. We found pictures of each of them and framed them. I think they were pleased and it set a good tone for the year.

We were off to a good start. Sister Robertine Bluth was a hardworking business manager. Margaret De Salvo was a quiet-mannered dean. May Jo Moran, who was new as Curriculum Director, was experienced as a SFA math teacher.

One of the first experiences was getting to know the senior class leaders before school even opened. Nancy Speaker, Barb Bayci, Beth Block, and Karen Plese were members of the class of 1979. Their moms had been my classmates and friends in the class of 1953. It was such fun seeing and meeting them. Karen Plese reminded me so much of her mom, Dorothy, that I actually guessed who she was before I knew her name.

Although I felt green and inexperienced, I was comfortable being back at the Academy. I knew the teachers, the parents, the parishes, the Academy history and the Joliet area. I was truly committed to SFA's aim of "graduating intelligent, Christian women."

"Jubilation" was a joint fundraiser for Joliet Catholic High and the Academy. The magnitude and spirit of the annual festival were awesome. Each year the project earned $100,000 or more and the individual talent seemed to multiply. We turned St. Francis Academy into a festival. Each of the 30 classrooms had a chair couple, who were generally parents who came up with a special theme for the

Glory be to the Father and the Son and the Holy Spirit. Amen.

The Annual Jubilation
S.F.A.-J.C.H.S
. joint fundraiser
transformed the
halls of S.F.A. into
"Broadway on Larkin"

Broadway Stars

Dale (Sr. Martha), Roy (Fr. Bob), and Trigger welcome all to the main show.

room. This included décor, talent, food, and drinks. There was a certain amount of competitiveness between them.

Certain ethnic groups were popular year after year, such as French, Slovenian, and Irish. Some rooms had themes, like "M*A*S*H." Customers were enthusiastic! Bob, Larry, myself, and the Jubilation chair people greeted every participant as we lined the doorway, squeezing each hand with the cacophony of "Thanks for coming!" "We appreciate you coming!" "Have a great time?" and "Welcome!"

Jubilation workers literally started planning themes and talent a full year in advance, so many of the Joliet Area Community businesses participated. Parents and friends would start putting up decorations at night while students were still having regular school the next day. The week before the opening, people all over town would say to me, "See you at Jubilation."

I had taught sixth grade medieval history for three years, and I remember emphasizing to my students that when a town built a cathedral, each worker took pride in his individual skill and the whole town participated. Watching the artists, electricians, and chair people working night after night reminded me of this phenomenon.

One of the first things I was warned about when becoming co-principal was to avoid promising anyone a ticket. The second thing I learned was that at the "Big Show" in the gym, Father Bob, Larry, and I would costume up to thank the chair couples and the workers. Shirley Smith, the artistic director, knew me and she would come up with the songs to sing. Once she dressed Father Bob and I as Roy Rogers and Dale Evans, and we sang "Happy Trails to You."

By years eight and nine of Jubilation, some of the enthusiasm began to wane. So in 1986, for year ten, we decided to celebrate the ten years and introduce the next fundraiser, Jubil-auction. That was in 1986. I think it is still going but always with a new slant.

Larry and I both thought that interacting with the students – knowing the product – was essential to our jobs so we were active. I moderated the yearbook. Larry helped with student council. We team-taught senior religion. I enjoyed it all. However, looking back, our teaching probably was a luxury considering we were both new in our administrative positions.

Sticking by each other's decisions was not always easy. Larry told the student council that as a drummer in a band, he had played at some great father-daughter dances that were similar to a prom. I thought that it should have some variety, like volleyball games or card-playing. The council disagreed, so we had the first "Pop's-and-

Pops & Lollies

Pop's 'N' Lollies
Father-Daughter Event
Wednesday
Nov. 22, 78
8:00-11:00
SFA gym
2.00 a person
music by
Bob Marcy
Orchestra

Deidre Streitz, '85, and her father-- King Pop and Princess Lollie

Larry brought his own little lollie

St. Francis Academy
Mardi Gras
FEBRUARY 24, 1979

Senior Class (No. 1 Sellers) of 1981
SFA's Annual Mardi Gras Fundraising Drive

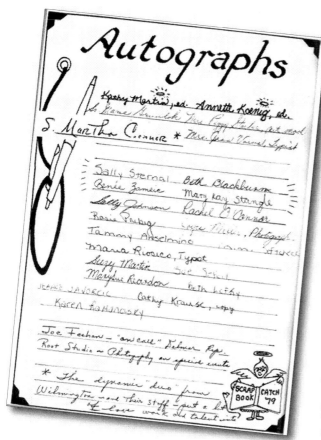

Co-Principals

From the 1979 S.F.A. yearbook I moderated

Lollies." I was wrong because the dance was wonderful! If the student didn't have a father, they could bring an uncle or someone else appropriate. Again, I think it is still going strong.

I always felt that my own SFA education was superb. We had great teachers and great classmates in a Christ-centered environment. We were taught to act out our faith. Once while I was teaching in Des Plaines, I said to Sister Mary Jean Morris, "They shouldn't allow SFA graduates to enter the convent!" I had just been told by my superior that I couldn't write to the television station to thank them for the wonderful coverage of Cardinal Stritch's funeral.

Larry and I were co-principals for two years. We exemplified what I often say about new teachers: "What they lack in experience, they make up for with enthusiasm."

After two years, Larry resigned. I'm sure that he had a variety of reasons. It was a good two years. The machinery of administration was getting clearer to me, and I was happy.

Sister Martha Connor, O.S.F.

Posing with daughters of Maureen Andrews, Dorothy Bajt, Natalie Jimko, and Mary Ann Stasko who graduated with me in 1953.

From the Principal. . .

Dear Alums, Parents and Friends,

Saint Francis Academy has an uncanny hold on me. When I graduated from SFA in 1953 back at Wilcox and Taylor, I walked across the campus and became a postulant the same year. Fourteen years later I returned to teach Theology and English at the new academy on Larkin. I had taught in Cleveland, Ohio; Desplaines, Illinois; Mansfield, Ohio and Chicago. But returning to my Alma Mater was very special and the seven years flew by.

In 1974 I once again departed SFA to work in the Pilsen area in Chicago with Mexican-American high school girls. Again it was a very satisfying experience. In February of 1978 I asked for a sabbatical to study Spanish and was told yes. But in March of 1978 I was asked to delay this and become principal of SFA.

So again I returned. These six years from 1978 to 1984 have unquestionably been the most professionally exciting years of my life. It is hard to put into words the thrill of being principal of SFA. You work with so many outstanding people.

But these six years have not dimmed my desire to have a sabbatical to study Spanish. So, on July 7, 1984 I depart for six months to San Antonio, Texas where I will be a student at the Mexican American Cultural Center. It is a program which includes Theology, language training, and skills to work with Hispanic people in this area. Second semester I'll study at a language institute in Cuernavaca, Mexico.

When I return in a year there is a good chance that part of my apostolate will be connected in some way with SFA. I have had the privilege of graduating from other great schools -Saint Patricks, Joliet; the College of Saint Francis; The University of Illinois; and the University of Notre Dame. But there is no school that gave me the sense of who I am and how I want to spend my life as SFA. Because of this, I will always be in touch.

The traditions of SFA reach back to 1869. Thank you for all you have done to keep SFA a vital excellent school. May our patron St. Francis give each of us the peace and joy his life exemplified.

If you get near San Antonio, stop by.

Vaya con Dios, *S. Martha Connor*

110

Kathleen Borio and I show off our look-alike smiles. Her dad is my cousin

Co-Principals

At a school assembly

Silver Jubilee

I desire that this renewal of my vows may be graciously accepted by the most blessed Trinity and endure forever, that it may be contained in every breath I draw, so that I may continue to renew it as long as I live, and keep it faithfully unto the end.

I acknowledge that I am too weak and frail to fulfill these promises. Therefore, I beseech Thee, good Jesus, who hast given me the will to make my vows, to grant me also the strength to keep them.

With my classmates at our Silver Jubilee

Charlie, Aunt Rose, Aunt Catherine, and Aunt Margaret, with me

With Sister Zita--our postulant mistress, at her Golden Jubilee

Ten

Silver Jubilee

In 1981, my fourth summer in administration at SFA, I celebrated 25 years as a vowed Franciscan sister with five classmates.

As I look at my Jubilee scrapbook, I think of Charlie's saying, "What is worth doing is worth doing to excess." Sister Mary Jean and I planned a retreat for our Jubilee class at Plano. We sisters owned a small cottage on a lake there. We brought food for meals, and asked a priest to say a mass. Each sister brought an activity to share relating to our jubilee.

I brought my 28 years of journals and went through them one by one highlighting passages and looking for patterns and themes. I didn't find the brilliant writing that I wanted, but I did discover two things: I got more honest and more selfish as the years went by.

Mary Jean wrote me a sweet note:

> Dear Martha,
> No matter what your journal says there are not
> many times you are ordinary. You are just very
> special. You have a charisma of leadership that
> is so fitting for one who is the "oldest" in our class.
> The honesty, the depth, the gift of yourself, shared
> this week and so often is a silver treasure.
> Love always, Mary Jean

June 27 was the all congregation celebration at the cathedral.

The Sisters of St. Francis
Of Mary Immaculate
Invite you to the Liturgy of the Eucharist

Celebrating the
Diamond, Golden, and Silver Jubilee
Of Religious Profession
Saturday, June the twenty-seventh
At one o'clock
Cathedral of St. Raymond
Joliet, Illinois

Lord, make me a religious according to Thine own heart, meek, humble, and obedient; a soul of meditation and of prayer; insensible to contempt, to injuries, to earthly things, and sensible only to Thy love and to the Holy Spirit. Amen.

The celebration was wonderful. The congregation served dinner at noon at the motherhouse, and the administrators served coffee.

At the cathedral celebration there were pastors, parishioners, and students from many of the parishes we served. The music of the sisters' choir was beautiful and stirring.

My friends, Maggie and Ed, watched the celebration with my godchild Brendan asleep on a blanket. Father Jerry Wagner and Father James Creighton, two of my Jesuit spiritual directors came.

The next day was a celebration, by invitation, just for me.

"I have cast my lot with the Lord"
1956-1981
You are cordially invited
To a Mass of Thanksgiving

Saint Patrick Church
710 W. Marion Street
Joliet, Illinois
Sunday, June 28
11:45 a.m.

Celebrant: Father Vytas Memanes, pastor
Cake & Coffee at 1 p.m. , St. Patrick's Hall
Cocktails at 3:30 p.m. at St. Cyril Convent, 664 Landau Street
Buffet at 4:30 p.m. at St. Cyril Hall
I hope you can join me – but I understand if it can be only in spirit.
Sister Martha Connor, OSF

The Mass at St. Pat's was joyous. I was in the church where I made my first communion, confession, and confirmation, and attended mass with my mother when I was a child.

My eighth grade teacher, Sister Rose Michael, who was an Adrian Dominican and had celebrated her 50th year as a sister, and friends from St. Procopius and from the parish were there too.

After the mass, I said thanks, and then I felt the need to say, "Being a sister is like other lives. On Monday, Wednesday, and Friday, I'm great, but the other days can be rough." I had to be honest. The rough and lonely days were mounting up.

Later that day, the sisters at St. Cyril and Methodius, the convent where I was living, helped me with an open house. This was planned mainly for my family, aunts, cousins, and special friends. I was starting to relax, and it was a lot of fun.

My Academy friends, Vicki, Mary Jo, and Mary Jane, bought me a bike. Judy Rogan McGuire and the St. Pat Class of 1949 gave me a gold watch and a travel certificate. Sister Marie's nieces made a beautiful pink and red quilt for me. It was all very humbling.

I remember while making my Jubilee plans, thinking, "I wish someone else would do all this for me." In the earlier days, all of the celebrations were planned by the superior at the motherhouse. Now we could plan them ourselves, and I felt lonely doing it. Father Mark Fracaro pulled the mass together for me.

I truly enjoyed my Jubilee. My motto, "I have cast my lot with the Lord," was true. But there was a decided amount of loneliness and turbulence mixed in. I had lost some certainty.

 My Dad (the lovable leprechaun) and Charlie, while I was teaching at St. Pete's, Mansfield, Ohio.

My thank-you card was printed with a picture of my dad, Charlie, and me at St. Peter's Mansfield.

Faith-family, Franciscan-friends

I believe that this snapshot from my days at St. Peter's, Mansfield, Ohio (1965) brings these themes together. I wanted you to have it because I think it also illustrates Fr. Jack's comments on my dad as the lovable leprechaun that he was.

You were, too, on my Silver Jubilee! Thank you for your generosity then, and for the day by day ways you enrich my life.

In St. Francis,
Martha

My Jubilee days were wonderful. When I look at my scrapbook, I still find joy in the words, "I have cast my lot with the Lord." It is just a new way to view my life.

1984-1986: As President ...

Looking very "presidential" as I answer the phone

1985-1986: S.F.A. gets a computer lab! Here I pose with the new word processing software....

we were even able to move all of the yearbook production to computer!

Lord
Jesus Christ,
Have mercy
on me,
a sinner

THE JESUS
PRAYER

Eleven

Principal and President

When Larry Johnson left SFA to work in marketing and fundraising, a decision was made to select an assistant principal instead of a co-principal.

I worked as a co-principal twice, and I know that it has advantages. However, it does take more planning time, and I was ready to go solo. The board hired John De Salvo who had worked for many years at Lourdes Academy, an all-girls Catholic School in Chicago, also operated by a Franciscan congregation. John moved easily into the position and was a great asset to the school.

My first year as a solo principal, I scheduled department evaluations monthly: September for the math department, October for the English department, and so on. In the midst of fundraisers and assemblies, I cherished the time I spent in the classroom. One of my professors at Notre Dame said, "If you don't put it on the calendar, it isn't going to happen," so I scheduled evaluations.

If I could single out a role of the principal that I believe is paramount to success, it is classroom visitation and teacher evaluation. I believe that a teacher is at his or her best while teaching. When I focused on this, I could be patient with individual idiosyncrasies. For example, a teacher might try my patience at a staff meeting but be very gentle with a student having difficulty with a concept.

This third year, I picked up a duty that Larry Johnson had done: attending the principals and coaches meeting of the Illini 8, which was our sports conference. Father Bob Colaresi, principal of Joliet Catholic High School, ushered me there. After the meeting, he always told me what really happened.

Sister Martha
...and Team

John De Salvo, vice-principal, Edward Russell, dean, Jeanne LeCuyer, business manager, with me as principal

Fr. Bob Colaresi, O. Carm., principal of Joliet Catholic High and I meet.

S.F.A. Angels Reach Final Four!

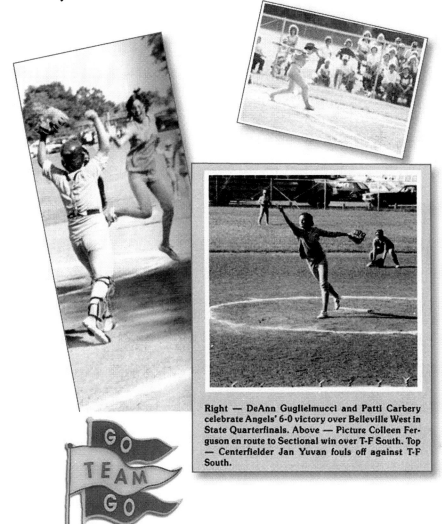

Right — DeAnn Guglielmucci and Patti Carbery celebrate Angels' 6-0 victory over Belleville West in State Quarterfinals. Above — Picture Colleen Ferguson en route to Sectional win over T-F South. Top — Centerfielder Jan Yuvan fouls off against T-F South.

GO TEAM GO

Remember, O most gracious Virgin Mary, that never was it known that anyone who fled to thy protection, implored thy help or sought thy intercession, was left unaided. Inspired with this confidence, I fly unto thee, O Virgin of virgins my Mother; to thee do I come, before thee I stand, sinful and sorrowful; O Mother of the Word Incarnate, despise not my petitions, but in thy clemency hear and answer me.
Amen.

One event I will never forget is the first time our softball team made it to the final four. Going down state to watch, I learned the importance of the pitcher. I became more familiar with parents and coaches. I saw the great importance in having a good coach. They had to know their sport, work the team hard, and be fair and kind at the same time. I came to realize how vital sports were to the players, their families, and the overall spirit of the school.

I hated to admit it, but I became a "jock" principal.

119

Reflection &
Spiritual Growth

KAIROS
(Greek for "time")
n. (KÎ - RÓS)

A specific period of time characterized by good fortune, urgency, and favorable opportunity.

A KAIROS moment is typically one which must be seized or it will be lost.

30

A moment of togetherness at Kairos.

Kairos Retreat: 3 days of fun and reflection at the Aylesford Carmelite Retreat Center in Darien

120

My admiration grew for coaches as basketball and volleyball got more competitive. I remember our basketball team playing in the huge University of Illinois dome in Champaign. Girls were getting scholarships to Georgetown and accepted into Harvard partially from their sports experiences. "Title IX" from the late 1960s was working. At SFA, we of course always had "equal time" for women's sports, but many co-ed schools didn't.

Due to the expanded curriculum we developed, this year at the Academy we had a greater number of male students for first period *Principal* classes from, JCHS, Joliet Catholic High School. Each morning *and* buses dropped off over 100 guys who were taking home economics, *President* advanced language classes, and band.

When the yearbook photographer was at school, I asked John and Ed to assemble the guys outside for a group picture. I imagined a quick snapshot of the boys standing on one of our grassy knolls.

Instead, Ed and John brought out chairs and bleachers and lined the students up carefully. I thought I'd never forget my frustration. I am sure that it was good for the school to have a balanced team: an intuitive woman helped by perfectionists. We had many laughs about our differences, but sometimes it was difficult.

Another change I was committed to was a three-day retreat for seniors. The "Kairos" retreat program for teens had been used JCHS. A team from a Jesuit high school near Chicago had trained their first team. Now JCHS trained a team for us.

It was a big undertaking, but SFA was blessed with dedicated teachers like Dan Roller and Sister Jeanne Bessette. *Kairos,* Greek for "a Christ happening," was based on the Cursillo Movement – a short course on Christ. Even good things are challenging, and I had to work with retreat leaders and coaches to make sure they weren't getting in each other's way.

I remember three particularly nice assemblies one year. One was for the 800th Anniversary commemorating the death of St. Francis. Father Charles Fasso, a very lively Franciscan came. A second celebration was for Bishop Imesch on his 25th Anniversary of ordination. We also had our first ecumenical celebration.

At another assembly, our head coach spoke to the student body to encourage attendance at our home games. Somehow one of his remarks upset our seniors and they walked out. I was horrified. Would this start a trend?

I ran out the front door to try to stop the exodus. As the seniors approached me, I held up my hands and said, "Please go back in, I

Times of Celebration......

We held an assembly in honor of Bishop Joseph Imesch: He celebrated the 25th anniversary of his ordination

Happy 40th Birthday, Mr. De Salvo!

want to announce the names of the seniors who are national merit scholars." They returned to their seats and I was so grateful.

Graduation was among my favorite events as proud parents and friends watched beautiful young women coming up the aisle for diplomas. John De Salvo would read the names from the pulpit, and I would hand the diploma to Bishop Imesch for presentation.

One afternoon in the midst of a graduation, Bishop Imesch turned to me and said, "Martha, you're cooing."

Principal and President

I was, and I loved being principal. I was less and less certain about my vocation. The nagging loneliness and confusion came out in my journal entries.

> *June 26, 1978*
> *11:00-11:30 p.m. – Bedroom*
> *I hurt so – going through such a depression – not sure whether I should fight or feel.*
> *Lord help me.*
> *My loneliness and vulnerability are overwhelming.*

> *November 23, 1978*
> *Today is Thanksgiving. I feel strangely "hurting" & strangely good and at peace.*
> *Karen Albert asked me if I'd be a nun again and I couldn't answer – I am quite sure that I would, but for some reason I find it hard to say it. I did tell her "yes" in a round-about way.*

Despite my interior storms, I forged ahead trying to be an excellent administrator. During the school year of 1982 to 1983, with the help of the staff, I wrote a detailed five-year long-range plan. It was grueling, but productive. I wanted it to be thorough and professional. Sister Ellen Doyle, a Franciscan sister, and Summer G. Rahr, a professional consulting firm from Chicago, were hired and established the guidelines.

I was to enlist 40 participants who would give a weekend to the pursuit. The group included teachers, parents, and alumnae, as well as outside resources. More than 70 responded. The participants were committed and smart.

O Lord Jesus Christ, who hast said: Ask and ye shall receive, seek and ye shall find, knock and it shall be opened unto you; mercifully attend to our supplications, and grant us the gift of Thy divine charity, that we may ever love Thee with our whole heart and with all our words and deeds, and may never cease from praising Thee. Amen.

Charge!

Boys Town

Hillmen invade S.F.A. for several classes. They can be found in Mrs. Burns' French IV class, Sr. Antl's Spanish IV class, Sr. Horak's Accounting class, Mrs. Welsch's Bachelor Survival class, Mrs. Murray's Band, and Mr. Downey's Choir. Angels descend upon the hill for one class, Mr. Anlauff's Physics.

Everything for the plan was open to discussion. The teacher surveys, for example, mentioned "more administrative leadership." And in spite of all the praise in the surveys, I'd be stung by some negative replies.

We ended up with 91 tactics to consider and implement for a better future. Many of them revolved around public relations, development, and recruitment. We had a blueprint for action and the implementation team headed by Jacque Marco forged ahead the following year. The 70 people who participated gave us their time and ideas, and I was so grateful.

Avis Clenendon, a Mercy Sister, gave an outstanding homily during Father Bob Colaresi's mass:

Principal and President

> *It is here where we ask the question – what do five-year planning, the cultural revolution, Franciscanism, think tanks, apples and IBM, holistic education, mega trends, feminism, advisory boards, mobilized funding, tell us about what God is doing? What does any of this say about God and the gospel?*
>
> *It is precisely here where we add the believer's data: God's Word; the Sacrament of Jesus Christ.*
>
> *We permit our work and our lives to intersect with God's word; the 114 year old story of SFA, the deep and abiding Franciscan dream and each of our personal stories to link to the Biblical Stories proclaimed at this point in our working the method.*
>
> *We give space and time for God's word to intersect this moment to confirm us, to challenge us, to console us, to insist we shape our vision in company with Jesus. Let our spirits here connect with the Holy One.*
>
> *And after we've done all our right and left hemisphere can do – after we analyzed, examined, and designed a preferred future – we turn it over in trust.*

Joliet's own Chicago Bear

Tom Thayer visits S.F.A., pictured with Chris
Reuvers, '86, and Karey Harvey, '87

One of my last letters to the participants sums it up. This was the first page of a full three ring notebook of all the surveys and new plans.

November 14th, 1983

Dear Bridge Builder,

Principal and President

When I look over the school year 1982-1983, my weekend with you was without a doubt both my best and hardest experience. I am deeply grateful for your time, talent, and honesty.

The weekend was hard because evaluating and planning is hard. It was great because we are about such an important human endeavor, the Christian education of women.

This book is an attempt to bring the weekend and the future plans together. Mrs. Jacque Marco and her committees are going strong on the 91 tactics we asked them to implement.

This book represents a mid-point in the process. I am proud to send you a copy of this, your work! Jacque Marco, Jean Vorva, and our staff spent days compiling it. I am very grateful.

Be sure to save Friday, June 8, 1984 for an anniversary event. It will consist of wine, cheese, and a report on what we have accomplished this year.

Hope all is well.

Gratefully in Saint Francis,
Sister Martha Connor OSF
Principal

Father Bob and I talked about the Jesuit Administration model which included a principal and a president. The importance of public relations and planned fundraising had become even clearer after the five-year plan. Most agreed that the role of president could be a great asset to the school, and the congregation approved the change.

I decided that the spring of 1984 would be my last as principal. People often asked me why I chose to leave SFA. The simple answer is that it is my nature to do a job and then move on; I get restless and look for new goals. I was convinced that the Catholic church

O Lord Jesus Christ, who when the world was growing cold, didst renew the sacred marks of Thy passion in the flesh of the most blessed Francis, in order to inflame our hearts with the fire of Thy love, mercifully grant that by his merits and prayers, we may always carry the cross and bring forth worthy fruits of penance. Who livest and reignest world without end. Amen.

Announcing the results with co-chairpersons Sister Lorraine and Sister Clare Wand

should be doing more for the Mexican-American community. I had permission to study Spanish and the Mexican-American culture in both San Antonio and Mexico.

Our board set up an interview process to find a new president, but it failed, although I'm not sure why. I think clarity and timing must have been elements in the impasse. I was asked to assume the role for one year. My biggest fear was getting in the way of the new principal John De Salvo and assistant principal, Sister Mary Rose Lieb, and I wasn't sure how I'd fit in.

For the first semester, I planned to study at the Mexican-American Cultural Center in San Antonio. I really felt that I should be out of the way. Pat McNamara, a parent, was one of the chair people of our elegant "Franciscana," which was held in November. He insisted that I return for the dance, and I did. Later I had a medical problem and preferred to have the surgery in Joliet. That ended the first semester.

The hysterectomy was uncomplicated, but I remember wishing I had a daughter to sit by my side. I had always been with my Mom when she was hospitalized. I had plenty of attention from Charlie and Alice, the sisters, and my relatives and friends. But I remember asking Sister Sue Bruno, a friend and former student, to please be "my little Margie." She assented.

I did not realize that after six years of being in charge at SFA, I would feel so isolated, and even useless. The administration, staff, and students were no longer my first concern, and I hated it.

Reluctantly, I directed my attention toward the alums and fundraising. Marianne Murphy, our new development director, set up meetings in California, Florida, and Arizona where Sister Anna Marie Becker and I introduced the alumnae to the current academy and its needs. I enjoyed meeting the alums. I knew many of them, and was always impressed with their caliber. I also learned to fall asleep quickly on our trips as "Annie" was a deep and constant snorer.

Marianne and I also put significant time into our first Harris Alumnae Directory. We had to go back 100 years. Marianne had been working to computerize alum files for months and she spearheaded the publication. The new Joliet Catholic Academy still continues this tradition.

Once again, I was asked to be president for another year, and I accepted. I tried to put together a slide show presentation on the Academy's foundress, Mother Alfred Moes. I even got to look at

Principal and President

129

S.F.A. and J.C.H.S. team up for SPEECH

architectural plans for the new Academy, which was to be built in the early 1900s. Mother Alfred had included both a bowling alley and an elevator, but this new school never was built.

Nan Clinton, a graduate, was our newly-instituted recruitment director. The enrollment increased. During my last year as president, Sister Vivian Whitehead, a friend and community leader, was on the board of the Joliet Spanish Center. The director, Neal Oaks, was resigning. "Viv" suggested that I might apply to be interim director, and I found the suggestion appealing. I had enjoyed great experiences doing a similar job in Pilsen. That December I was chosen by the Joliet Spanish Board of Directors to be the director. So I worked at SFA in the mornings and at the Spanish Center in the afternoons.

Being fearless, courageous, and naïve are closely linked when it comes to my own personality. I soon found out that the Mexican-American Community in Joliet was very diverse. Many families had been in Joliet for generations, some were from Texas, while others were from Mexico. Their needs varied, and I felt overwhelmed.

The Spanish Center was located on Eastern Avenue and had been St. Mary's School, where I had attended first grade. The building had served Joliet's needs for exactly 100 years. So I had a celebration.

Joe Adler informed me that the Spanish center had opened through the leadership of Catholic couples in the 60s. The purpose was to help immigrant workers who had come to Joliet to work on the farms be able to settle down and establish a life.

It was a painful time because I did not feel particularly effective as president of SFA. Now I also felt that I needed to plan to resign from the Spanish Center because its needs were beyond my skills.

Principal and President

Regarding SFA, my counselor said that after eight years in administration and seven before as teacher, that the leaving should actually be a time of reflection and celebration. It was up to me to make it happen.

I planned a mass of thanksgiving and a Sunday brunch for all of the people who had helped me. I invited those who helped with Parent Board, Jubilation, Franciscana, the five-year plan, alumna officers, booster club, and bingo.

The day was filled with sunshine, and the chapel looked beautiful. After the mass of thanksgiving, we came downstairs to Alumna Hall, where our food service had prepared a lovely brunch.

I was happy because along with a general speech, I was able to individually thank each person.

The room was filled with parents I had met at all these events, the Sisters from our congregation, administration, Father Bob, Larry Johnson, and my family. Some people even turned the tables on me and offered their appreciation of my work.

I knew that I also needed to plan for my resignation at the Spanish Center. I had a part-time assistant who spoke Spanish fluently, and I decided to ask the board to appoint him as an interim director, which I did in mid July. Then called friends and found an opening for an English teacher at Holy Trinity in Chicago.

I knew the Holy Cross brothers, who ran Holy Trinity, from my summers at Notre Dame. I admired them and thought I was ready for another stint in Chicago's inner city.

I had learned the lesson of anonymity during my first year teaching at St. Jude's in Cleveland. Now, after being principal and president of SFA for eight years, the lesson was even more painful as I returned to Chicago, and once again, this came as a surprise.

Twelve

Years of Turbulence

Leaving Joliet in July 1986 pushed me into a four-year emotional turbulence that I still find painful to recollect. Reading over my journals from those years, I realize that I was like an exhausted swimmer trying to get to shore.

There was turbulence before, but this time, there were no familiar elements like the Academy and friends, the sisters I lived with, my brother, and my family. I was alone in unfamiliar territory.

In the late 80s there were no longer preordained convents. Sisters were allowed to live in groups of two, three, or four; and even alone if there was a good reason. My decision to move to Chicago in late July was sudden. Sister Mary Lou Marchetti knew of a nice vacant apartment near her on Magnolia Street in Uptown, and I took it.

My brother, my nephews, and my cousins usually helped me move. Looking back, these turbulent years resulted in ten moves. At the top of this long stairway to the back of my apartment, I could look west and see a very large city cemetery which reached all the way to Western Avenue.

I had an eclectic collection of furniture. I had a kneeler (pre dieu) from the Guardian Angel Home. I put a big plant on it just as I had in each of my previous residences. My couch was covered in orange-plastic, similar to those in waiting rooms, so I covered it with a spread. Maggie Phair gave me drapes. The apartment had wonderful light and was quite comfortable. I have no idea where I got the nice dining room table and chairs. My friend, Don Roller, gave me a marble end table. I still have it.

Holy Trinity High School was a friendly place. I had visited it the previous year with a group of Mexican-American students from the Academy. My friend, Brother John Tryon, taught there and arranged a religious discussion with eight of his students and mine. The day was a success because the students enjoyed meeting each other. Many exchanged telephone numbers.

The faculty was a wonderful mix of religious brothers and sisters and young dedicated laymen and laywomen. I was very comfortable with my fellow staff, but teaching was a different story. I taught two classes of seniors, a freshman religion class, and a study hall. I foolishly thought that it would be an easy year because I wasn't responsible for administration or fundraising,

The student body was largely made of black and Hispanic students and the other students were mainly first or second generation Polish. My textbook for senior English was *English Literature*. I had taught the material many times and was not worried, but at the quarter, one class's grades were five A's and ten F's. I knew that should never happen! How could the material be that easy or that hard? I knew that I was to blame. Without meaning to, I was detached from the school. I was realizing that this would not be a long-term position for me.

The students were great individually, but somehow as a group, they baffled me. I hadn't found a way to teach effectively. I remember when one of my English students who was black, sat down near my desk and asked me if my family was prejudiced. He was sincere, but I did find the question a little unnerving, and I had no good answer. He wanted to know why all white folks were so prejudiced. I explained that my Mom and Dad hadn't seemed prejudiced, but that I had an aunt that had taught in Chicago who did.

Later, I worked with addicted city workers at Parkside Addiction Center at Little Company of Mary on the South Side, where about half were Irish Catholic and half were black Baptists. I met whole families and I gained a feeling of comfort. I realized that I could have called mothers, fathers, or grandmothers for assistance in getting assignments at Holy Trinity done.

But despite feeling ineffective for the third year in a row, I was my true self in many ways. I was in charge of faculty birthday celebrations in our break room. Also, despite warnings by the assistant principal, Brother Ken Haders, I had said "yes" when students asked me to moderate a talent show.

Credo
I believe in God, the Father almighty, Creator of heaven and earth and in Jesus Christ, His only Son, our Lord; who was conceived by the Holy Spirit, born of the Virgin Mary, suffered under Pontius Pilate, was crucified, died, and was buried. He descended into hell, the third day, He rose again from the dead. He ascended into heaven and was seated at the right had of God. From thence He shall come to judge the living and the dead. I believe in the Holy Spirit, the Holy Catholic Church, the communion of saints, the forgiveness of sins, and the resurrection of the body and life everlasting. Amen.

Holy Trinity had a nice auditorium where I often watched talented students practice in the afternoons. One girl who sang had groupies and a manager; and another group of senior boys lip-synched Michael Jackson, complete with grabbing their crotches. Although I pleaded, I knew that the grabbing would happen during the performance. So with input from the administration we hoped that one performance after school and one at night would settle the problem. Suddenly, I knew why Brother Ken had warned me!

My uptown neighborhood, Broadway at Lawrence, felt like inner city. There were many stores and apartment buildings and very little grass. Most of the restaurants were Asian and very good.

The first morning in Chicago that I drove to Holy Trinity down Lawrence Avenue, I had to slow down my car. Two women had run out of an apartment and were brawling in the middle of the street. Traffic went around them, and finally a guy from the same apartment complex came out to stop them.

My teaching day was the least of my problems because I came home from school to a very empty apartment. To lengthen my day, I started driving home via Claybourne and Ashland and found health food stores and a good dry cleaner. I also joined Women's Workout World. Then one day a young couple with a baby moved in next door. The baby's name was Jimmy, and he had dark curly hair and was about ten months old. His mom let him play in my apartment each day for a little while. I had a few visitors, especially from Joliet, but the emptiness grew.

Unfortunately, my migraine headaches were constant. My neurologist at Rush St. Luke Hospital thought I needed some relaxation therapy. I agreed and found myself going for sessions with two young doctors. The relaxing techniques were good but they asked me some questions which made me pause. "Do you have any intimate friends – i.e. anyone you talk to everyday?" I didn't. Later, mulling over the question and answer pulled me into a lonelier place than usual.

My therapist, a rabbi, and my Joliet neurologist discussed hospitalization for my headaches. That frightened me, and I asked Charlie and Alice to come to my next session. The therapist agreed that I was not ready, but Charlie and Alice thought that the Pritikin Center in Santa Monica would be a good choice for Christmas break. Dr. Pritikin taught the importance of healthy, low-fat eating, and the center was a wonderful setting with the exercise, lectures, and walks on the beach. Also, I got to see my niece, Tracy.

Neurologists, therapists, Pritikin, retreats – gave me insights and hope, but the unrest, loneliness, and headaches continued.

I even lost the element of brightness I had come to expect in my days. My little neighbor Jimmy and his parents moved away, and their apartment stood empty.

The years leading up to my departure from the convent were a constant struggle, but my year on Magnolia in Uptown stands out. I was so happy when two other sisters living in Chicago suggested that we rent a house for four or five sisters for the next year.

The house on Hood Street was about 20 blocks north of Lawrence and Broadway, near Broadway and Bryn Mawr. The house had a brick front and was long and narrow. It was good to be living with sisters once again on a street with yards and flowers. The teaching at Holy Trinity, however, actually got more difficult the second year. So when Tom McCabe, a friend from Joliet, called me to say that he was the director of a new hospital unit for adolescents with addictions, I was very interested. It was a Parkside Unit, under the auspices of Lutheran General Hospital.

So during my last semester, I worked from 8:00 to 1:30 at Holy Trinity and then at Parkside from 2:00 to 5:00. My job at the hospital was to tutor hospitalized high school students and to coordinate their studies with school personnel.

In August of 1988, I made a workshop with "Hood Street" for one of our sisters, and it also fit in with my new position at "Parkside". The workshop was called "Family Recovery" and was designed for personal and family growth, and for understanding the full scope of addictions.

August 17, 1988

I begin my new journal at 6:55 a.m. in a quiet chapel – alone with the Lord. The chapel is cool, I am awake and I feel in tune with the Lord and with the world. Thank you Jesus! I am at a family recovery program sponsored by Parkside.

Yesterday I was speaking with Sally Manning and when she told me she was studying to be an Episcopalian priest, my "heart burned within me." The thought of being an Episcopalian priest sounded so good to me that it frightened me. I will start by praying and making some inquiries.

I know why it was so exciting to me – it would be a way out. I could be in ministry – and have a "legal" way for leaving the convent. This was one month before I asked Sister Vivian, our president, for a one year leave of absence to live "out of the convent" while still legally a part of the community.

I had been struggling with this since age 40, but actually saying it made my head spin and my heart hurt. Sister Vivian knew me well and was very kind. She explained the papers I would have to sign for Rome and the Joliet Chancery, and told me I would need an approval visit from a priest. This was all good, and I actually I felt that it was a procedure protecting sisters from a mid-life crisis or worse.

I never thought that I would leave the convent. I had given my word. I had made a vow.

How could I leave?

When I told my spiritual director, Father Don Kenny about my plans, he seemed surprised. Since I had left SFA, I hadn't seen him regularly, and I think he wanted to make a last attempt to guide me.

My last therapist, Dr. Kanter, told me that probably I would always be a "square peg in a round hole."

Sister Elizabeth Marie cried, and my brother Charlie and my friend Mary Jo Burns were also sad.

I had always thought I was raised "Nunny." Being Catholic had always been important to me, and I always knew I'd be a teacher.

On October 8th, 1989, I left the convent. When I was ready to leave, Sister Vivian said, "Martha, when you came to the convent, you had 'pomp and circumstance.' I think we should have a little departure ceremony." I invited my family and my closest friends, Over 20 people came.

> *October 9th, 1989*
> *Yesterday I signed my papers from Rome – it was a long hard day.*
> *At the ceremony at 11:00 a.m. in the boardroom:*
> *Charlie and Alice, Cele, Libby, Olga, Suzanne, Marie, Pat Kilbane, Mary Jean, Alfie, Sue Bruno, Mark Fracaro, Bob Colaresi, Therese Griffin, Elizabeth, Viv.*
> *At the Holiday Inn: Pat Lev, Ann, Maureen, Danny.*
> *Libby said, "Everyone should give thirty-five years to humanity!"*
> *Cele quoted a priest, "When you fall on your face and get up, you're a full length ahead."*

136

Bob said that the Joliet Catholic Academy is more
of a reality because the Carmelites trusted me.
*   I cried and said that there was a lot of pain and a*
lot of peace. Suzanne and Pat drove me in and back.
I'm exhausted – to bed.

The Sisters of St. Francis
of Mary Immaculate

Years of
Turbulence

I had been fighting leaving for so long, and was relieved that I had finally left the convent.

Although the next year is a blur, it included an inspirational pilgrimage to Israel with Father Bob Colaresi and thirty others, helping Charlie with an unsuccessful campaign, being broke and taking a job at Truman College which entailed teaching English as a Second Language in the morning and a writing class in the afternoon.

The headaches continued to increase. My neurologist suggested giving myself shots of medicine; the initials were DHE. I started taking this powerful medicine, but the headaches kept returning. When I went to the Diamond Headache Clinic, my doctor strongly suggested hospitalization; I finally gave up and consented.

It felt like I was going into a detox clinic. They had a medical staff that taught about different ways to deal with migraines, and I was on a hospital floor with thirty other people who all had severe migraines. They first weaned us off all our medications. For the first two or three days, I was in a daze because my head was pounding and they wouldn't give me anything significant for the pain.

That was one of the lowest points in my life because I was taking time off from work and I was hospitalized. I was sick, broke and in a Jewish hospital over Christmas! I remember on that Christmas Day, a deacon came in to give me communion. He was Korean. It was like an apparition of angels, and I was so grateful to receive the Eucharist on Christmas morning.

When Father Bob and I were principals, we shared our doldrums with each other. One day Bob told me, "You crawl out faster than I do." I'm not sure why. I think sometimes that I am just being practical. There is always so much to do.

During my time of turbulence leaving the convent, I started making collages which cheered me up and gave order to my life. This was my first one. It is a collage of smiling faces.

On that Christmas day in 1990 my brother Charlie came to visit. He is so loyal. Then my cousin, Pat Levandowski, and her daughters Mary Kay and Ann came. The visits brought sweetness to the day. I truly believe that saying, "God writes straight with crooked lines."

During my time in the hospital, I had a chance to talk with the staff psychiatrist. He said something that seemed strange to me: "If the nuns had wanted you to stay, they could have kept you." After telling him about my money problems, he suggested that I find someone who would loan me money when I needed it. So, I asked Alice's mom, Libby, and she agreed. I never borrowed a large sum of money from her, but she helped me out many times during my first few years out of the convent.

My work with Parkside included four sites and the last was a hospital on Chicago's South Side called Little Company of Mary. There were nuns and a chapel, and I felt at home. Things continued to get better. Although there were still high waves, I had found a shore.

*Collage of silver jubilee celebrations for my priest friends,
Fathers Tony, Mark, and Bob above.*

Celebrating my friends.

*God,
come to
my assistance.
Lord, make
haste to
help me.
Glory to the
Father,
and to
the Son,
and to
the Holy Spirit;
as it was
in the beginning,
is now,
and will be
forever.
Alleluia.*

Jimmy is in the second photo in the first column above.

Olga is receiving her medical degree in the largest photo below..

Meeting Gloria was so much fun!

Years of Turbulence

During the "turbulent" years of post-nunhood. I attended many friends' weddings

Thirteen

Desert Storm and Power Dating

If I had children or grandchildren, one healthy habit I would try to pass on is keeping a journal.

My sophomore religion and English teacher, Sister Jean Paul, initiated this concept, but not until I entered the convent did it become a consistent habit for me.

By consistent I mean that I always have a cloth-bound book so that I can't rip out pages. I use it to record events, to write out my feelings, and to write "Letters to Jesus."

I make two or three entries a month. I have my parents' deaths chronicled as well as the day I left the convent and many world events.

In my 40s and 50s I'd make lists of things that upset me. Once I hit 13 and called my therapist. So the second healthy habit I'd try to pass on is to always have a therapist. I use mine like I use a dentist. When the pain or confusion builds, I call for an appointment.

The third way I use my journals is for "Letters to Jesus." Quiet prayer is difficult for me, so often when I'm reading scripture or other books, I stop to write.

While rereading my journals from years 1989 to 1992, my "Power Dating" years, I noted that I always stayed current on world events.

June 5, 1989
An incredible weekend world-wide.
Russia – 800 killed in railway accident.
Poland – voting victory for Solidarity.

Beijing, China – army kills hundreds in student
protest for democracy.
Khomeini dies, the people mourn in a frenzy like manner.

I had three entries for world events:

January 16, 1991
A bit before six o'clock Charles W. called and said,
"Turn on the TV – the war has begun." Television was
covering the war before the White House announce-
ment came around 6:10 – Bush will address the nation
at 9 p.m. Sister Pat called and I said – "Come down."
We both watched. There is something so unreal about
this – there are correspondents in the enemy territory
– Desert Storm.

March 9, 1991
Thank God – the war is over! I think March 2 or 3
– such celebration – homecomings – flags and yellow
ribbon all over – wonderful but Saddam Hussein is
still in power in Iraq.

December 21, 1991
Today the Soviet Union was demolished!
Wow – what a year.

After rereading my journals I separated my dating methods into
four categories – computer dating, fix-ups, newspaper ads, and running into. I don't know if there are any books on Power Dating over
50, but I think I could add a chapter.

I would emphasize that dating can be difficult. If a guy was interesting, I'd be nervous. If he wasn't, the evening would be long.

I'm not sure why I believed that I would meet the perfect man
and marry him within a year, but I did.

What was clear to me was that I wanted a husband, because loneliness was the biggest factor in leaving the convent. I was never very
popular with boys in high school, so what did I think had changed?
Part of it was being a principal. I was used to interviewing teachers
and making assessments, and I saw dating as a series of interviews.

Great Expectations, a dating service, was my first avenue for dating. I lived in an apartment complex in Chicago where periodically there would be flyers in our mailboxes. One was for Great Expectations. I guess it was a 1989 forerunner to Match.com. I called and made an appointment for an interview. Because I was nervous and anxious, I arrived early. In the same near-north section of Chicago was a new micro-brewery. It was brand new and quite welcoming. It had high ceilings and tall plants. A huge operating brewery was enclosed in glass in the center of the restaurant. I was very impressed.

Desert Storm and Power Dating

I sat down at a side bar. I never liked beer, so despite the place, and all the special brews, I ordered a Virgin Mary. It was late afternoon, and an official looking man in a suit stood near smiling. I complimented the décor and asked if he was one of the owners.

He said he wasn't, but that he was the brew master. After my Virgin Mary betrayed my lack of interest in beer, we chatted and then I excused myself for my appointment.

"Come back after your appointment and I'll buy you dinner," he offered. I answered, "Maybe."

This proved a major theory of mine. When I take action, good vibes surround me. Before I had even interviewed at Great Expectations, I had a date.

This dating service was quite an endeavor. The office was a suite of rooms on the second floor of an office building. A lovely young woman took me into a comfortable sitting room and started the interview with a question, "What would you consider a pleasant date?"

"Dinner and a movie," I responded.

The questions continued, and the information she gathered was rather generic, but the procedure was very clever. Each participant received a four-digit number to protect last name, address, and phone number. For an additional fee I could get a glamour shot, but I just brought a picture I had.

The data I submitted was typed up and my picture was placed on the top left of the page. Everyone's sheet of information went into a binder like a catalogue. I was on the "woman shelves" under "M" for Margaret. They also videotaped a segment where I described a pleasant date. It was incredible. There were binders upon binders in separate libraries for men and women.

The interviewer suggested that I come in at least once a month to look through the catalogues and fill out a minimum of five postcards. This always took me less than an hour. I would select a binder and flip through it. I found someone age appropriate every ten or fifteen pages. I would read his description briefly, and then unless he seemed totally into hunting, fishing, and camping, or a self-proclaimed atheist, I'd write down his number.

These postcards were sent to the five selected men with my name and telephone number. The men could call me, go to the Great Expectations office and check me out in the binder or on video, or ignore it.

At the same time, I received the phone numbers and names of the men I had selected. Either person could initiate the call. I generally waited. Out of five cards I'd submit, I'd generally receive two calls.

I thought that these were pretty good odds. The fee was at least $200 or $300 hundred dollars. This was good because as a result, only people who were truly interested joined and their privacy was protected. My first Great Expectations date was a charming Latino man who was a superb dancer and could cook. He was perfect, except for his diminutive size and his eagerness to settle down. He was very flattering, and said that as his first date, I more than made up for his joining fee. I had actually found someone lonelier and more eager to marry than I. We dated two months.

My other Great Expectations dates weren't so eager. One was a Ph.D. from the University of Chicago who was fun, but quite stuck on himself. I think he was used to dating co-eds. He had a bachelor buddy who had just been married, and this may have been his motivation to start looking.

He'd often call on Saturday mornings to chat and ask me about different restaurants around Chicago. Since eating was a major hobby of mine, and I had lived in five or six different neighborhoods in the city, I was knowledgeable. It finally dawned on me that he was asking me for restaurants to which he was taking other women. We had two dates.

In between, I was seeing the Brewmaster I'd met in the new bar. He had lived around the world and was truly a lady's man. He had great lines, and I fell for him, but not enough to stop using Great Expectations.

The next two gentlemen I dated were from the northern suburbs. One was retired from the telephone company, was Catholic and had a great home. I was very interested. On the second date I met his daughter and went to mass with him. But I don't think he was attracted to me; he is the only one that I think toyed with me. Although I still have a recipe from his daughter, two dates it was.

My last Great Expectations date was a gentleman who was only allowed to drive to and from work because of DUIs. He operated heavy equipment on highways for the state, and he was "on the wagon" whenever I went to dinner with him. We'd always go to Red Lobster and a movie. I was so insulted the first time I went out with him when he requested two senior citizens tickets. I was 56 or so. However I've never paid full price since. He was an easy friend. He was divorced and lived close to his ex-wife and children. We enjoyed each other, but neither of us were interested in anything more. I saw him once a month for about six months.

Desert Storm and Power Dating

My friends knew of my Great Expectation dates by the monikers that I gave them: Heavy Equipment, The Brewmaster, Latin Lover, and Professor.

I also met men through friends, which proved to be the worst way. My sweet niece, Tracy, knew a wonderful guy through the Chicago drama scene. The arrangement was that I would join her as she met a group of friends at a comedy club, and then go out and eat.

Tracy's friend was nice-looking and very cordial. Because we both liked Tracy, we were both very sweet to one another. Tracy kept glancing over to see how we were getting on, and I think she was disappointed when we didn't exchange phone numbers. There was nothing there but mutual respect for Tracy.

My next "fix-up" was through a woman I'd met in a Spanish class I was taking. Again, I think she had us meet at a comedy club with her husband and her.

My date was an accountant from Sri Lanka who was younger and much thinner than I, but he was charming, complimentary and loved teaching me geography. He was taking classes to become a travel agent.

I was dating him when I had to be hospitalized for my headaches. He came to visit me while I was off my medication and rather groggy, and he brought me a World Atlas which I still have. He was very nice. I'm not sure how this ended; perhaps because I moved away from Chicago.

One Sunday afternoon while I was staying with my friend Suzanne, I decided to answer newspaper ads. This third dating strategy was most economical.

The ads resulted in three dates. One was a part-time coach who was a charming alcoholic, one was a butcher who was very religious, and the third was a retired gentleman who wore tennis shoes with his suits. These were all one-date specials.

Generally, the men I ran into seemed more interesting. The first was the brewmaster, and the second was a teacher.

While I was working for Parkside Addiction at Little Company of Mary Hospital, I gave a talk at a Catholic school for boys. One of the teachers asked me for a business card. He wanted to discuss a student with me. His questions lasted about two months. He was attentive, and I enjoyed him in my life, but this ended abruptly when he finally mentioned that he was in the midst of a divorce.

When I realized that my Parkside job was dependent on insurance, and that Little Company was considering changing to an outpatient service, I started looking for another job.

I got a further administration certification at a college on the South Side. My professor was a former school superintendent with lots of expertise. I received the certification and started sending out résumés. This process was more discouraging than looking for a husband. I sent out dozens of résumés and got only two replies. One day I stopped to see the professor for some advice. He asked if I liked music, and I did. He had tickets to a concert that weekend. He picked me up and gave me a set of vacation photographs to look at while we drove to the junior college in DuPage. He traveled the

United States extensively. When we arrived at the concert, he explained the type of orchestra and the selection of music we were about to hear. I felt like I was on a school field trip. But when we arrived home, he gave me a quick kiss, and I decided that it had been a date.

Because of his interest in education, politics, and religion, we had great debates, but he made it clear that he would never marry again. He had lost his wife two years earlier. Of course, I thought I could sweep him off his feet, but I didn't. However, he was a great friend.

I believe that everyone past age 50 is interesting, at least for one date. I agree with the Biography Channel: "Every life has a story."

I had not yet come to Lincoln and had not met Jack, but I believe that the joy of meeting Prince Jack was enhanced by all the toads I had to kiss first. This was about to happen!

Desert Storm and Power Dating

Prince Jack awaits

Ginny, Laura and staff gave me a shadowbox of memories .

My beloved friend, Jackie Thornton
Aways helping others and lifting spirits
Makes great pumpkin pies

150

Fourteen

Lincoln and Logan

I came to Lincoln for money and stayed for love.

Though working for Parkside was great, I knew that the insurance for inpatient care for teens with addictions was a tough sell. Outpatient services was the preferred way for HMOs. I didn't think my position had a future and that it would probably be phased out.

An ad in the Chicago Tribune for an Educational Administrator at Stateville with a $60,000 to $70,00 salary looked exciting.

Coming from Joliet, a prison town, Stateville didn't terrify me. Still, my cousin Jerry Levandowski who worked at Stateville was horrified because Stateville housed the toughest criminals.

I applied a week later and was invited for an interview with John Castro, the Assistant Superintendent of Correctional Education for the State of Illinois. Going through the prison halls with gates clanking behind me gave me only small reservations.

I felt strong in the interview. Yes, I had worked with adult learners. Yes, I had taught black, white, and Hispanic students. Yes, I had taught at grade school, high school, and college levels and had worked in a Spanish center, addiction center, and had an addiction certification.

I did not realize how slowly the state moves with good jobs. It seems that the church and the state are powerful, chauvinistic, and do important life-saving work. They also take their sweet time about it all. In both cases I feel their tasks are worthwhile and essential.

I visited my friend Rosemary Morrissey Ahmann's mom who still lived on Briargate Avenue in Joliet. Margaret Morrissey had worked for Warden Reagan at Stateville while Rosie and I were still in high school. She was also an early warden at Dwight Women's Prison. Margaret asked me, "Who is sponsoring you?"

She then explained that it would be both smart and necessary to have someone with political clout put in a good word for me. My brother, Charlie, was active in Republican politics, and he offered to call someone in the Secretary of State George Ryan's office.

I eventually got a call that a Ph.D. candidate from Chicago got the job at Stateville, but I was asked to consider a similar position in Lincoln, Illinois. For a state job with a good salary, I would go anywhere for a while. The place I was offered was Logan Correctional Center, a co-ed medium security prison.

It took months to finalize my job, even months to be called for required blood and urine tests. But one day John Castro finally called asking me to begin work.

The move to Lincoln was financially and physically tough. I was moving to a city at age 54 where I did not know a soul and would be working in an entirely new institution, a prison.

I asked a moving company if they could transport me to Lincoln on a Sunday. They said that they would and mistakenly gave me an estimate for Lincolnwood, Illinois. When I told them, "not Lincolnwood, but Lincoln, Illinois," they were very concerned. The price went up substantially, and they weren't even sure that they had jurisdiction to drive to Central Illinois.

I quickly learned that it took money to have my phone and electricity installed. I lived on my Shell Gas credit card for weeks. What the Shell Mini-Mart didn't carry, I didn't eat. The irony was that I had to drive fifteen miles to get it.

I began my eight year run at Logan Correctional Center on July 27, 1992. John Castro brought me to Logan for my first day and invited all the teachers to meet me in the training room. I met the Adult Basic Education and General Efficiency Diploma teachers whose work stretched from level zero through 12. The college vocational and academic staff were also present. With directors, there were 20 people in the room.

I greeted everyone, but I'm sure that my fear showed. I stayed in a room at the Lincoln Holiday Inn my first week. One night, I ate a whole plate of cookies that the culinary arts teacher gave me.

As paperwork for the state is notorious, I spent hours with Gail Hunter, acting principal, Greg Firkus, assistant warden, Jim Chrisman, the principal at Lincoln Correctional Center, and Pat

Murphy who directed the McMurray college Program at Logan. Springfield staff from District #428 helped me too.

Sharon Schoof, Greg's secretary tried to keep me on track. I came in every Saturday for the first six months trying to understand the system and keep up.

In my new contract, I was listed as Chairman of Inmate Literature. I thought that this was because I had a master's degree in English. It should have been listed as Porn Specialist. When an inmate received magazines which were pornographic, they went to a committee of one – me! This was not a priority with Gail or my predecessor, so drawers in a cabinet were filled with these magazines.

None of the magazines were in general circulation. If a magazine could be sold in a store like Esquire or Penthouse, it didn't need to be checked. The magazines that I checked were from adult book-stores, and I couldn't just say yes or no.

Each magazine had to be assessed page by page. Regular nudity was okay. Sexual intercourse was okay if it wasn't brutal, bestial, or with someone dressed as a corrections officer.

The form I had to complete was tedious. If on page three of a magazine, there was a picture of brutal sex, I had to specify that. If a magazine was okay except for a few pages, I would rip out the un-acceptable pages and approve the rest. If too many pages were unac-ceptable, the warden or assistant would dispose of the magazine, or at the inmate's request, return it to the sender.

In either case, I would have to send for the inmate and explain.

I did this paperwork on Saturdays so that no one wandered into my office.

After I got caught up, I asked the librarian, Pat Kirby, to look at the magazines and fill out the forms. She was generous and efficient. The task was easier. All I had to do was see the inmates. Porn was 98 percent of the materials checked. Other books were confiscated if they were questionable – like how to make a bomb.

One of the most exciting aspects about being principal of the prison was finding out what a great educational system the State of Illinois had. The Illinois legislature along with the leaders of School District #428, the district which included all the correctional cen-ters in the state, actively built programs.

The school was housed in a modern program center with ten well-lighted classrooms. This was a whole new group of students.

*Feed the hungry
Give drink to
the thirsty
Clothe the
naked
Shelter the
homeless
Visit the sick
Visit those in
prison
Bury the dead*

CORPORAL
WORKS
OF MERCY

Chaplain Henry Johnson surrounded by his wife and teachers at his retirement celebration at Rusty's restaurant

I made a plan. I went from room to room greeting individual teachers and the classes, and asked the students to continue doing their individual projects. Then, I went from desk to desk quietly asking inmates their names, where they were from, and if they liked math or reading better. I repeated this in the afternoon with the women's classes.

After a few days, the inmates became another set of adult learners to me. The correctional officers gently teased us. Officer Reed Leamon said, "Margaret, you are turning these guys from blue collar crime to white collar crime."

Lincoln and Logan

But during my eight years at Logan Correctional Center, more than one officer said to me that if it weren't for the teachers, there would be no rehabilitation.

When an inmate entered the system he or she took a basic education test and received an equivalency score. Sadly, the average grade level was 4.0.

If inmates scored below 6.0, the Illinois legislature mandates that they receive 90 days of classroom education. Some inmates welcomed it, many fought it – but generally, it happens.

The teachers had incredible stories. The basic education teachers have had to teach the alphabet.

All of the teachers were certified – some had master's degrees and I had one teacher who had his doctorate. I initially questioned his decision to go by "Dr. Maus." But it worked for him. His students admired his background, and I think it inspired some inmates.

The teachers like most teachers, were concerned about their students at test time. I remember sitting around our convent community room at St. Pete's Mansfield, Ohio while we corrected papers. "Is this all they learned?" was the going complaint.

It was the same at Logan. When a student missed on his GED exam or didn't test out of mandatory education, the teachers would get so discouraged.

Being a prison educator had joys and sorrows. Most regular teachers get affirmation from students, families, and the community they serve. Prison educators get questioned about helping criminals.

But prison educators saw their jobs as very rewarding. They knew that many of the students had never had a quiet classroom. When they started to improve their reading and math, they got excited and so did the teachers.

I loved the *Autobiography of Malcolm X*. As an English teacher I particularly appreciated the chapter where he described learning

After my first cancer, I went back to work at Logan looking like a mummy

faith

My dear friend, Jaquie Marco, died of cancer in 2003 but lived beautifully 'til the end

the entire dictionary. He had been a bright student in grade school. When he got to prison, he realized how poor his vocabulary was. He couldn't read the books that he wanted.

A nurse found a dictionary for him, and he tediously began copying and learning a page a day. His vocabulary grew to the point that he sounded like a professor the rest of his life.

Because of this, when the professor I was dating from Chicago who ran the community spelling bees suggested that we have a spelling bee at Logan, I was interested. The assistant warden gave me permission, and we launched the first Malcolm X Spelling Bee. My friend, Charlene Young, is still the chairwoman. I believe that they are on the fifteenth competition. All the teachers work on it, and cheer for their individual students. There are even prizes.

Although I am sure that some of the teachers thought my ideas were juvenile, they did cooperate.

Logan Correctional Center had an annual graduation coordinated by the veteran college director, Pat Murphy. MacMurray College of Jacksonville, Illinois granted the degrees. The GED graduates were awarded certificates of completion at the same event. The short length of many prison terms meant that two thirds of the GED graduates had gone home before the annual celebration. *Lincoln and Logan*

As principal, I set up quarterly graduations which corresponded to our testing times. I wanted to celebrate each student who got his GED and each student who completed his mandatory education achieving a 6.0 level. This was also a time to thank the teachers.

Warden Bosse and assistant warden Greg Firkus attended because they both saw education as a way out of the system. Tammy Smith and her culinary arts class baked a big cake.

The GED graduates had a chance to share a few words. The inmates would thank their teachers and encourage the inmates who had just received their 6.0 certificates to keep going in school. This tradition continues.

Once, an inmate was in my office, and I had his high test scores in front of me, I acknowledged that he was good in school, and asked him why he didn't get a job and stay out of prison. He looked at me in exasperation and said, "You don't get it lady, I'm a criminal." He was blond and looked like he had been a model for a Norman Rockwell painting, and I was to believe that he chose bank robbery as his lifetime profession.

A tough part of working with inmates was that half of the time they told the truth, and the other half, they were spinning me.

How is a principal of a prison school different than being a principal of a Catholic high school? What struck me as a nice difference was that I didn't have to worry about enrollment or budget issues, which were paramount in a private school. And of course, there was no need of parent nights or alumnae meetings. What was the same was the biggest challenge in every school, keeping the teachers and the bosses happy.

During my fifth year as principal, I got two commendations. One was in an article in a correctional magazine that named Logan as

Happy Retirement!

THE BEATITUDES Blessed are the poor in spirit, for theirs is the kingdom of heaven. Blessed are those who mourn, for they shall be comforted. Blessed are those who hunger and thirst for righteousness, for they shall be filled. Blessed are tho merciful, for they shall obtain mercy. Blessed are the pure in heart, for they shall see God. Blessed are the peacemakers, for they shall be called sons of God. Blessed are those who are persecuted for righteousness' sake, for theirs is the kingdom of heaven.

My retirement from Logan Correctional Center

Celebrating with Sherrie - in the white suit.

158

having an educational program that worked. This was due in large part to the veteran educator, Pat Murphy, who coordinated the college program. We were both thrilled.

The second was from an Illinois college study group that assessed pre-parole programs. It stated that Logan had a good program previously, but under my leadership it had improved to number one.

"Pride goeth before a fall." That same year, I was demoted.

I knew that I had made some serious mistakes, but had accepted reprimands and thought that all was well.

In coordinating the pre-parole program, I had kept a female inmate working through the lunch period. Generally there is plenty of food, but this day the menu was fried chicken which only happened once a month. I felt so badly that I stopped at a fast-food place on the way to work the next day and bought chicken for her.

I knew that I was breaking a rule, so I told her to eat it quietly. Instead, she took the chicken to her unit in the bright wrappings. Giving anything to an inmate is strictly forbidden, and I was written up by an officer.

The other two infractions were more innocent and less blatant, but I realized that I better be more diligent. Either I was getting too comfortable, or was being watched more carefully.

It is still painful for me to recollect the announcement. We had a celebration at Logan for the 25th anniversary of District #428, and as I was walking back to the program center with two of the school administrators, the assistant warden invited us into his office. After he closed the door, he said something like, "Margaret, have you thought about going back to teaching?

I was stunned, but I did figure it out. The topic was open to question and debate, but I was not up to that. I think I responded, "If you have lost confidence in me, then that's it!"

I was embarrassed, hurt, and angry. It was hard to believe. We had just been celebrating together.

I took a sick day and drove to Evanston to see my counselor, Kathy Huston. She listened, then said very clearly, "Margaret, you still have a job. Do you realize how many people your age are just let go? It happens all the time. Go back, be sweet and thankful."

It was not what I wanted to hear, but it was true. I could have been fired over my mistakes. Administrators don't have unions.

The transition took weeks, and I did not publicly discuss it. Eventually, I got my new assignment and new work hours. Being there from noon till 8 p.m. made it easier on me, and on Gail who

Lincoln and Logan

Blessed are you when men revile you and persecute you and utter all kinds of evil against you falsely on my account. Rejoice and be glad, for your reward is great in heaven. We all want to live happily; in the whole human race there is no one who does not assent to this proposition, even before it is fully articulated.

FROM THE GOSPELS OF MATTHEW AND LUKE

159

was the new principal. Gail and the teaching staff were kind to me. I had sent them each a letter shortly after it happened, weeks before the actual change so they wouldn't be surprised.

My first night class of pre-GED was horrible. The class was used to Gail's teaching style and was not happy with mine. The other class was Cooperative Work Training Skills. I had a dark classroom in an old wing of a workshop.

But in the great "yin and yang" of life, at the same time, I was totally preoccupied with becoming Mrs. Jack Peifer. The wedding plans lifted my bruised spirits.

Top left is Margaret Morrissey who was superintendent of Dwight Prison and my mentor

Fifteen

Jack, Langston, and Cancer

Once my relationship with Jack was serious, people would always ask, "Where did you and Jack meet?"

Since Jack was 55 years old and a confirmed bachelor known as a regular churchgoer, faithful to his widowed mother, and diligent at farming – people were surprised at the turn of events.

I'd smile and say, "Where else? I met him in his living room."

This was the wonderful truth. When I accepted the position at Logan and moved to Lincoln, I did not know one soul. Sister Margaret Duffy told me that Mother Immaculate's sister lived in Lincoln. So, when I registered at the Catholic parish, Holy Family, I asked Monsignor Goodman if he knew this particular lady, and he did. Her name was Helen Peifer, and he called her on the phone.

I took the phone and explained who I was and that Mother Immaculate had been my first superior. Helen said, "yes" when I asked her if I could stop by to see her.

The following Sunday, I drove out past Lincoln Christian College and found her home. When Helen came to the door it was like seeing Mother Immaculate in a pretty dress. We sat in the living room and began sharing convent stories. Helen introduced me to her son, Jack, who was sitting on the other side of the room in his Sunday best, smiling. He mainly listened in the background as Helen and I exchanged anecdotes. I didn't pay much attention to Jack during the first visit, as I was still dating the professor from Chicago.

Helen and I continued speaking on the phone weekly. Shortly after we met, she fell and broke her arm, so I'd stop by on Sunday with a cake or a pie from the grocery store.

On my first New Year's Day in Lincoln, Helen and Jack took me out to dinner in Mason City. When Jack came in the front door, he was wearing a brown tweed jacket, a yellow shirt and a tie, and his big smile. I looked twice! This guy was really good looking. Why hadn't I noticed!

While at dinner, I told Jack and Helen that I was hoping to buy a condo and stop renting. When Jack drove me home after dinner he told me that he would be glad to help me when I moved. I thanked him not realizing that when he'd help me move into my condo on Railsplitter, that he'd become a permanent part of my life.

On March 19, 1993, Jack came with his big red truck. Our first stop was at the home of the Bailey family who had sold me the condo and some furniture. Jack loaded it on the truck, but there were some large glass pieces so I had to ride in the back of the truck holding them in place. It was cold, and I wasn't wearing gloves. It was only five blocks away, but I complained loudly. The event yielded one of our first good laughs.

We didn't stop working until noon. Helen had prepared salmon croquettes and au gratin potatoes for us. We enjoyed the food and returned to work.

At four o'clock, my friends from Logan, Jeanette, Wayne, Charlene, Jim, Randy, Greg, Dennis, and Sharon came to visit. Jack told Charlene to run to the store for cheese since it was a Friday during Lent. At five o'clock, Jack told me that he was leaving to feed the cows.

I walked him to his truck and thanked him. I told him I was grateful for helping me and for being with me all day. He smiled, leaned down and gave me a perfect kiss! I was pleasantly stunned.

After that day, whenever I wanted to see Jack, I'd call and say to Helen, "Can Jack come over to hang some pictures?" The next winter, Jack volunteered to paint the lower level of my condo.

Eventually I wrote to the professor to tell him that I was dating a Lincoln farmer. I thanked him for his friendship and told him that I understood from the start that he didn't want a committed relationship. It seemed a gentle farewell.

He wrote back asking me a series of questions. Then I wrote to him saying that if he wrote again I would consider it a proposal of marriage or sexual harassment. I didn't hear from him again.

Jack had started his quiet march right into my heart.

At the same time, I discovered a new passion. I had invited Paul Gleason, a local historian, to give an educational in-service on the history of Lincoln to the teaching staff at Logan. It was a Friday afternoon, and my mind began to wander. Suddenly I heard Paul say, "And Langston Hughes wrote his first poem here in Lincoln."

My head bolted upright. Was Paul on something? Langston Hughes, the poet laureate of the Harlem Renaissance, had a connection with Lincoln?

Paul was right of course. When Langston was the class poet at the new Lincoln Central Junior High, and the assembly hailed his graduation poem, he came to a major decision.

One biographer and friend, Milton Meltzer, put it this way.

> *To hear him tell it, it was not his own decision, but his classmates' that started Langston Hughes writing poems. He was about to graduate from grammar school. The students had elected all their officers except the class poet. They were stumped because none of them had ever written a poem. One thing they had learned, however was that a good poem has rhythm. So when someone yelled out his name, the vote went unanimously to Langston.*
>
> *He was fourteen then. He had never thought of being a writer, but he did not refuse the honor. He wrote sixteen verses in praise of the teachers and his class.*
>
> *Langston Hughes enjoyed telling the story about the odd beginning of his poetry. He liked to leave the impression that if he hadn't been applauded at graduation, he never would have had a first poem.*

I was excited about the story of Mr. Hughes, but when I found out that he continued to write to his eighth grade English teacher, Ethel Welch, for thirty years, my heart pounded. I was convinced that this was a man and teacher for Lincoln to celebrate.

The stars were aligned. Our chaplain, Henry Johnson, became involved in the project to honor Langston. He informed us that the high school had signed copies of first editions of Hughes' works. Henry's wife was a high school English teacher and had seen them. Langston had sent his books to Ethel Welch with personal inscriptions. They were found in a bottom drawer.

I learned that having a celebration for someone famous to the community is a good way to meet interesting people.

Hold fast to dreams
For if dreams die
Life is a broken winged bird
That cannot fly.

— Langston Hughes 1902-1967

Richard Sumrall, the librarian, hosted a Langston exhibit. He enlisted Russell Allen, a library volunteer, to find evidence that Langston Hughes actually graduated in the first graduating class. When Russell found the list in *The Courier*, the local newspaper, we found another great surprise. Jack's Uncle Frank, who was Helen's big brother, was in the same class.

People were interested in erecting a historical marker. We formed a committee called Friends of Langston. The first donations came from clergy, Glen Shelton and Norman Goodman. Helen Rainforth and Sam Redding, business people, hosted a party. The fifth graders at Central School led by teacher Joe Hackett, performed Langston's poetry. The *Courier* with Nancy Saul and Ann Klose covered the event. The organist at Holy Family, Tim Woods, wrote a musical composition to the poem "I've Known Rivers." Lincoln college hosted speakers. The backing was spontaneous and somewhat overwhelming.

My eighth grade teacher, Sister Rose Michael O.P., often used the metaphor, "Life is a tapestry." She taught us that, "We are weaving a tapestry day by day and that the full beauty will only be shown when we finish and see the other side. Dark threads, our painful days, will enrich the final piece of art."

In 1994, I was falling in love with Jack, working on a plaque for Langston, and life was good.

But one afternoon, I received a call from my sister-in-law, Alice. There was panic in her voice. "Muggs, Matt has melanoma. Would you call your friend at the Mayo Clinic in Rochester, Minnesota?"

My niece, Darcy, Matt's older sister and a physician, had found a doctor at the University of Michigan in Ann Arbor, and I called David Ahmann in Rochester. I told myself that Matt was young, healthy, and a fighter and that there are many advances in curing cancer.

When my friend Rosemary handed the phone to her husband, *Jack,* David, I told him about Matt. He quietly asked questions. Then he *Langston,* said that the University of Michigan was a great place for Matt to be. *and* He welcomed us to Rochester, but informed me that Matt's condi- *Cancer* tion was very serious.

That is not what I wanted to hear, of course. I wanted to hear that Mayo had cured many cases just like Matt's. But I listened to what David was saying.

The next Sunday morning at mass while I was singing, "You may cross the barren desert, but you shall not die of thirst," I began to cry. I was overwhelmed with grief. After mass, I stopped to see a friend. She told me that my faith was strong, and that God would get me through my sorrow. I realized that faith was not enough.

I realized that I needed professional help.

I called the hospital for information about cancer support groups and was given the name of a counselor, Dee Stern. Dee didn't have a magic wand, but she gave me assignments, which seemed to help.

I told her of how kind and smart Matt was. She asked me if I had ever said that to Matt. I hesitated, then replied, "I think he knows."

Dee asked me to write a letter to Matt telling him how special he was to me. It was difficult because I didn't want to embarrass him. I wrote the letter anyway and have always been glad that I did.

Matt had private time with each of his siblings. He traveled to Saipan to be with John. He stayed with Ted in San Diego, and Tracy in Los Angeles. Tracy arranged for a back stage visit with Jay Leno. Matt also spent time with Darcy, Richard, and their three sons in Portland. The siblings refer to this as Matt's goodbye tour.

Matt saw numerous doctors. Charlie and Alice stayed close to him. Their agony was palpable.

I believe that Matt was the only one that didn't deny the fact that he was dying. He was proficient with the computer and studied everything. His last stop was at the University of Illinois Hospital in Chicago. He was there about a month.

The Late 1980s

Our Father who art in heaven hallowed be thy name. Thy kingdom come, thy will be done on earth as it is in heaven. Give us this day, our daily bread and forgive us our trespasses,as we forgive those who trepass against us, and lead us not into temptation but deliver us from evil. Amen.

John, Tracy, Ted, Darcy, and Matt

Matt loved his brothers and sisters

166

The final surgery lasted only thirty minutes. The melanoma was in his brain, and nothing could be done to help him. Charlie and Alice were scheduled to take Matt to yet another specialist in Los Angeles. They held on to the hope that another doctor could help. I called the siblings and suggested that they come to Chicago. Ted made arrangements. I remember picking up Tracy, Darcy, and Ted at O'Hare. Darcy said that flying into Chicago had always been a happy time; she was coming home. This time was painfully different.

*Lord I believe
Help Thou my
unbelief*

PETER

I believe that John arrived from Saipan the same day.

After two and a half years, Matt was in his final hours of life.

The siblings sang, read aloud, and prayed.

A decision needed to be made about life support. Ted gathered Grandma Libby, cousin Jenny, Charlie and Alice and the four siblings at the apartment that Charlie and Alice had rented near the hospital. I remained with Matt.

I sat by Matt praying and telling him that he had our permission to go to God. I held his hand and told him how much I loved him – how much we all loved him. Even though Matt was confused, parts of his memory responded. He joined me in singing "You Are My Sunshine" and "On Top Of Old Smoky."

My heart was breaking and the time seemed long.

The decision to allow Matt to peacefully die by removing life-support systems was momentous. Ted had gathered everyone in a circle and they said "The Our Father." One by one, each shared a decision. Charlie was last.

They made a courageous decision, and returned to the hospital.

I ran. I told myself that the whole family was there, so I could go home to Lincoln and back to work. I knew I was running. The family kept vigil with more singing and praying.

The next afternoon, I got the message that Matt had died.

Charlie encouraged me to come to Joliet that night. I got to Grandma Libby's before the rest of the family arrived from Chicago. Their entrance was so sad. As I hugged each one, we cried.

Planning the funeral, the two-day wake, and the funeral mass where each of the siblings took part filled our time. Support from friends and relatives helped us through the next four days. Bagpipers welcomed Matt's body at the cemetery.

Charlie and Alice memorized the remarks of parents who had also lost a child. They included, "God will not forsake you." "Time will be your friend." "Part of it gets harder as time passes."

167

Darcy with baby brothers

Darcy comes home from Portland with Grandson # 1,

Ted with John and Matt

Uncle Matt loved his nephews, Alec, Rocky, and Connor

Alec

Connor

Rocky

168

In Loving Memory of Matt Connor

CONNOR, MATTHEW CHARLES
Age 24. Tuesday, February 4, 1997 at University of Illinois Hospital at Chicago. Survived by his parents, Charles and Alice Connor, of Minooka, IL. Two sisters, Tracy Connor of LosAngeles, CA and Doctor Darcy Martin of Portland, OR; two brothers, Ted Connor of San Diego, CA and John Connor of Minooka, IL. Also survived by his grandmother, Elizabeth Scriba of Joliet; an uncle, Allen Scriba and an aunt, Margaret Connor of Lincoln, IL. Also survived by his fiance, Sarra J. Kleban of LasVegas, NV. Preceded in death by his paternal grandparents, John and Anne Connor and his maternal grandfather, Robert Scriba. Matthew was born in Joliet and graduated from Eisenhower Academy, St. Patrick's grade school and Joliet Catholic High School. He graduated Magna Cum Laude in Electrical Engineering from the University of Notre Dame in 1994. Memorials to the Melanoma Research Foundation, 2834 West Nasa Blvd., Webster, TX 77958 would be appreciated. Visitation will be held at the Fred C. Dames West Chapel, corner of Black Road and Essington Road in Joliet, from 7-9 p.m. on Wednesday, February 5 and from 2-5 and 7-9 p.m. on Thursday, February 6th. Funeral services Friday, February 7, 9:15 a.m. from the West Chapel to St. Mary's Catholic Church in Minooka for a Mass of Christian Burial at 10 a.m. Interment Elmhurst Cemetery, Joliet.
FRED C. DAMES WEST CHAPEL
3200 Black at Essington Rd., Joliet
For information, 741-5500

Jack, Langston, and Cancer

Matt, age 4, typical pose

Proud family with
Matt at his gradu-
ation from Notre
Dame: John, Alice,
Matt, and Charlie.

My funny, brilliant,
& kind nephew Matt

In the midst of Matt's illness, I was diagnosed with cancer.

I went to Chicago to visit my friend Bobby and celebrate my friend Lorette's birthday. On Saturday, I had my hair cut in the big city. Sunday morning as I was scrutinizing the cut, I felt a lump on my neck below my right ear. There was no lump on the left side.

Though I was concerned, it was Sunday, and I was going to a party. On Monday, I called my doctor who scheduled an appointment with an ear, nose, and throat specialist.

The specialist said that he was 99 percent sure that the lump I had was not cancerous, but that it should be removed.

Jack, Langston, and Cancer

Jack took me to surgery. When I came out of surgery, I asked Dr. Philip Garcia if I had cancer? When he answered, "It's not conclusive." I knew that I did.

Jack's and my relationship developed during the year. I was dependent on him, and he was so responsive. The day I came home from the hospital, he came over to fix my bandages. He was so gentle.

I was 60 and had a good life. Matt had just graduated from Notre Dame in electrical engineering and was 21. My cancer was treatable, and I wanted to exchange my life with his.

Jack, the staff at Logan, my family, and friends were so supportive. I was able to work through my chemo and radiation.

I was on a three week treatment cycle. I had treatment late on a Thursday afternoon, then would crash Friday through Sunday. I was able to work on the following Monday. During the first week after treatment I might have to leave work early. I'd have a relatively easy time for the following two weeks. Then, the cycle would begin again.

I was glad that I could work because I had just bought my condo, and I had meager savings. Making house payments motivated me.

One morning while I was limping down the stairs with a charley horse and holding my aching, bald head, I grumbled to myself, "Margaret, you've got grit."

The chemo treatments were rough. I would get nauseated and a bit high. My memory was affected. A teacher visited me at Christmas and brought a gift, and I totally forgot.

God takes care of me. Having Cindy, a friend from Logan, and her baby Jesse live with me those months was a consolation. Jack continued to help me through my cancer and Matt's death. Our love was deepening each day. Jack loved me even with my bald head.

Jack's HOLLYWOOD Years

A Star Family

Take #1972

Jack with his parents

When our courtship was in its fourth year, and Jack had not proposed, I considered moving north. I even applied for a job. Because Jack was concerned for his 92 year old mother, he was hesitant to move forward with me. But, I found that I couldn't leave Jack.

I was deeply in love. I loved Jack and would never leave Lincoln.

I never wanted to be without Jack's presence. He was a man of quiet action. He courted me by coming to my condo unannounced. I would look out my window and see him shoveling snow or weeding a flower bed. Once when a friend stayed overnight and was about to leave, I looked out and Jack was scraping snow off her car.

Jack, Langston, and Cancer

Sometime in late October, my friend Bobbie came to stay with me after my cancer surgery. On Halloween, the doorbell rang accompanied by loud knocking. When I checked, there was no one at the door. As we closed the door, Jack stepped out of the bushes wearing a black mask. His costume was his army uniform which still fit. When he left, Bobbie remarked, "He is so good looking. How did he escape marriage?" I hoped to change that.

Jack looks like a cross between Henry Fonda and Jimmy Stewart.

The year, 1997, was a year of great tragedy, and also great joy. We lost Matt, and it was the year that Jack discussed our engagement and a ring.

Because of Matt's illness, I was with my family almost every week. Alice and her mom, Libby, thought that Jack was perfect and encouraged me to keep dating him. Even my nephew, Matt, joined the chorus.

Jack knew that I wanted to get married and thought that a ring might calm me down. Alice found a perfect diamond solitaire at Teak's Jewelry store and wanted Jack and me to look at it. We did.

On February 2, 1997, two days before Matt died, Jack and I became engaged.

Peifer Reunion at our farm

Our handout at the Peifer Reunion

The Peifers' of Route 10

July 22, 2002
Jack's 65th Birthday

Jack's first home . . . 1936-1938

Henry 1903-1978
Helen 1904-1998
Jack 1937
Margaret . . .

Aunt Kate & Jack - 1943.

Fr. Claude Peifer making sure that Jack says "yes." - 1998.

Jack, his Farmall & McCauley Kids - 2001.

Their Hollywood years 1940.

Henry - 1977.

Tom & company enjoy roast.

Ann Mosier instructs Margaret - 2002.

Peifer Reunion - Jim & Angie - 2002.

The Peifers gather on our front porch during a reunion

Jack,
Langston,
and
Cancer

Jack...

Jack with great-nephew,
Jack Connor

Sixteen

The Wedding

"This is the day the Lord has made – let us rejoice and be glad." Jack surprised and delighted me when he woke me up with these words.

I had stayed overnight with Helen and Jack because my house was full of wedding guests, and I wanted a quiet night.

My high school friend, Sally Carey, had come from Kansas City to be my chosen mother of the bride. My niece, Tracy, came from California to be my personal attendant.

Although the wedding had been planned in just seven months, I tried to think of every exigency. I knew that Sally nurtured me even in high school, and that Tracy made soups that calmed and nourished. They both helped me.

Many others also helped. Patty Peifer took care of the altar flowers and corsages. Father Mark helped me plan the liturgy. Our organist, Ruth, played and accompanied the soloists.

Matt's girlfriend carried a candle in the offertory procession, which Matt had given me for Christmas the year before.

I also had my two godchildren, Tricia and Brendan, carry up the water and wine. My third godchild, my great nephew Alec, was only four, and didn't participate. My friends, Loretta Pavlik and Sister Marie Grunloh, were Eucharistic ministers.

Because of our ages, 62 and 60, we thought of having a small wedding, but no one liked that idea, and the wedding list grew.

Whenever Jack went to the grain elevator for business, he came back with another name for our guest list. Everyone wanted to see the bachelor farmer take the plunge!

Jack is blessed with many cousins. He also had an uncle and two aunts who were still living and would attend.

If I speak in the tongues of men and of angels, but have not love, I am only a resounding gong or a clanging cymbal. If I have the gift of prophecy and can fathom all mysteries and all knowledge, and if I have a faith that can move mountains, but have not love, I am nothing. If I give all I possess to the poor and surrender my body to the flames, but have not love, I gain nothing. Love is patient, love is kind. It does not envy, it does not boast, it is not proud. It is not rude, it is not self-seeking, it is not easily angered, it keeps no record of wrongs. Love does not delight in evil but rejoices with the truth. It always protects, always trusts, always hopes, always perseveres.

I had the McCauley clan, academy friends, work friends, Connor cousins, priests, and Franciscan Sister friends.

We easily had 300 invitations.

We wanted to get married on Valentine's Day, which was a Saturday that year, but we had started our planning too late.

We chose the following Monday, President's Day, February 16, 1998, which we thought was significant because of living in Lincoln, Illinois.

We used a red, white, and blue theme at the reception. A teacher friend, Laura, lettered our invitations. My friends Reed, Charlene, Mona, and Evelyn cooked and arranged the rehearsal dinner. Reed grilled steaks. As Jack is a member of the Knights of Columbus, we had the dinner there. The dinner alone grew to a party of fifty. Many of my out of town guests had not met Jack, and I had not met all of Jack's cousins either.

After Jack awakened me on our wedding morning, I went to get my hair and make-up done. I already had a French manicure with hearts on my ring fingers.

Of course, I wanted a perfect dress for the wedding. I had seen a dress in a Talbot's catalog with a white lace top and a black skirt, and thought it was perfect.

After I received it, I realized I was wrong. The lace looked like a cheap kitchen curtain, so my cousin Rosie helped me. She took me to a bridal shop where I kept asking for mother of the bride attire. I finally ordered a blue satin dress.

Then I ordered a dress from JC Penny. Nothing seemed right.

Cousin Rosemary also insisted that I register at JC Penny for dishes and houseware. She wanted to have a shower for me.

The shower was fun – we did not play any games.

I cancelled the blue satin dress, sent back the Talbot and JC Penny dresses. Ten days before the wedding, I found a perfect white silk suit with beading at Von Maur's in Bloomington. There was a beautiful large white hat with black ribbon that seemed a nice complement. I felt very comfortable and pretty in it.

Jack wore a tuxedo and was as handsome as ever.

After we took pictures at church, we visited Jack's mom, Helen. She was not strong enough to go to the church, but Mona, one of her caregivers, dressed her and curled her hair. Helen's dress was a beautiful rose silk, from Von Maur's. Helen looked beautiful, and we put on her corsage. We have some wonderful pictures with her.

The Wedding Mass was at one o'clock. We got there early, checked

178

on a few things, and started to await the guests back in the sacristy. Tracy quotes me as suddenly saying, "I can't stand it. I can't wait back here." Out I went with Jack to the doors of the church to welcome all of our visitors. We had our reception line first. It was so informal and fun.

My brother Charlie and his wife, Alice, were our attendants. So at one o'clock, Charlie and Alice started down the aisle together. Alice looked great in a bright red, wool suit with a matching hat, as did Charlie in his tux. They entered the church smiling and set the tone for a joyous celebration.

The mass and wedding ceremony lasted an hour and a half.

We had two special homilies – one was by my friend, Father Bob Colaresi, who was known for his colorful deliveries. He roasted me and encouraged Jack, and people laughed.

After the mass, Father Claude Peifer, a Benedictine scholar and cousin of Jack's, gave a historical look at the Peifers in Logan County. I found out I was not the first Margaret Peifer. (See appendix for both speeches.)

We drove thirty miles north to Jumer's Chateau in Bloomington, Illinois for the reception.

The bar was open and the buffet was ready.

We wanted the celebration to continue seamlessly. So as soon as people found their tables and had a drink, we commenced the typical ceremonies.

Sister Mary Jean, my friend and president of the Joliet Franciscans, offered grace.

Our cake ceremony was next. There were three cakes. Jack's uncle, Vince, and my cousin, Rosie, each had a separate cake, as February 16 was their birthday. So we cut three cakes.

We sang to Uncle Vince and Rosemary, then had our first dance.

The room was quiet as they enjoyed the full buffet.

I had read in a bride's book that Erin Brennan had given me, that a table for two was a smart way for the wedding couple to have time with each other and avoid the formality of a head table. So Jack and I sat together and the toasts began.

My niece, Tracy, was the emcee. Jack was the first to speak. He read a letter I had written to him on Sadie Hawkin's Day in which I had proposed. I was embarrassed, yet pleased that Jack had saved it.

Tom Peifer had secretly handed out fifteen keys to women at the reception. He called me forward then said, "Jack, your long years of bachelorhood are over, so girlfriends of Jack please return your keys to Margaret." I was flabbergasted when the many female friends came forward.

My friend Cele shared our long history. She said, "Margaret entered the convent, and that was good. Margaret left the convent, and that was good. Margaret married Jack and that is very good."

Ed Russell, friend and co-worker at SFA, said, "only Martha could get you to drive 100 miles bearing gifts on a free day."

My Chicago pals, Mary and Suzanne, read fake telegrams from dignitaries around the world congratulating Jack and me.

My brother Charlie shared a story about walking three miles to see Grandma Connor where I talked the entire way and never noticed that he had not said a word.

Dancing, conversations, introductions, and much joking and good wishes continued until finally only a few of us were left. John and Loretta Pavlik were staying overnight at Jumer's, and Jack and Ann Kane's car would not start.

We stayed in the bridal suite at Jumer's. Jack served me coffee in bed from our room service tray. To this day, he still brings me coffee in the morning.

We had two days in Chicago and two days in East Moline. The honeymoon was short but sweet. In Chicago we stayed at the Hyatt Regency and went to a Bulls' game on Michael Jordan's thirty-fifth birthday. Dennis Rodman and Scottie Pippen also played. Jack loved the cheerleaders, the Lova-Bulls! You do not get to see them on television. In East Moline, we visited the John Deere Historical Museum and Corporate Headquarters. Jack knew the history of most of the tractors.

We saw the movie, *Titanic*, on our honeymoon, and for three nights I dreamed about drowning. The fact that the heroine Rose continued calling for the hero Jack, haunted me.

Jack and I had gone together almost five years before we got married. I tell everyone, "It took me five years of hard labor to get him down the aisle, but it was most definitely worth it."

Jack and I with the Connor family

The Wedding

Rehearsal Dinner

Chicago buddies
Suzanne & Mary

With Cele

SFA Classmates who came to celebrate my wedding

The Wedding

I pose with cousin Kay, seated, and her three beautiful daughters who came to the shower. I taught Kay for
three years at the Academy. She is acting director at
Carpenter House for the homeless

Cutting the cake
at rehearsal dinner

The Ceremony

Charlie & Alice ↗

Sharon & Bea

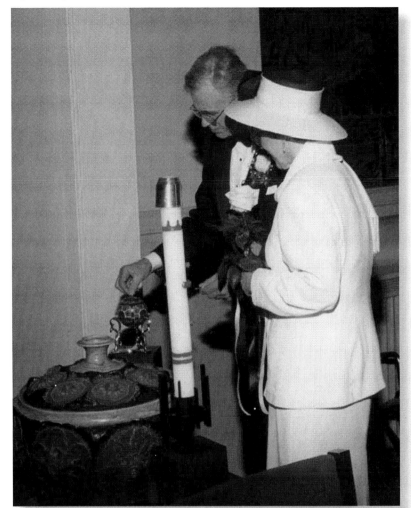

The Wedding

Fr. Bob, Charlie, & Ted

Beaming with Joy

With Jack and Libby

The Wedding
Couple

Margaret & Carm with Jack and Me

....the Reception

Tracy and John

The Wedding

Lorette & John

Mary Jo
& Fr. Mark

S. Cathy & Fr. Bob

The Celebration of

The Sacrament of
Holy Matrimony

Uniting

Margaret Mary Connor
and
John Henry Peifer

Monday, February 16, 1998
Presidents' Day
One o'clock p.m
Holy Family Church
Lincoln, Illinois

Concelebrants of the Mass:
Father Mark Fracaro
Father Tom Mack, Pastor
Father Claude Peifer, O.S.B.
Father Bob Colaresi O Carm. · Homilist

Jack's family has worshiped here for 150 years. Margaret joined the parish 5 years ago. We welcome you and invite you to greet one another, sing and pray with us.

Jack and Margaret

Wedding day with Helen
Darcy's husband Richard took the photo

At the reception: Fr. Mark, Vickie, and Mary Joe

Our first dance
"May I have this dance for the rest of my life"

WEDDING

Margaret and Jack

Connor-Peifer

Margaret Connor of 2340 Railsplitter Ave. and John Henry Peifer of 1495 State Route 10 were wed on President's Day, Monday, Feb. 16, 1998, at Holy Family Church.

Margaret is the daughter of the late John and Ann Connor, who lived in Joliet. John's parents are Helen Peifer of Lincoln and the late Henry Peifer.

The wedding Mass was concelebrated by the Rev. Tom Mack, the Rev. Claude Peifer, cousin of the bridegroom, the Rev. Bob Colaresi and the Rev. Mark Fracaro.

Charles P. and Alice Connor, brother and sister-in-law of the bride, attended the couple.

Jim and Tom Peifer and Greg Morrow, cousins of the bridegroom, and Ted and John Connor, nephews of the bride, seated the guests.

Following a reception at Jumer's Chateau in Bloomington, the newlyweds left for a wedding trip to Chicago and Moline.

Margaret is a graduate of the University of Illinois in Champaign. She is an educator, employed by Logan Correctional Center.

Jack, who graduated from Lincoln Community High School and Lincoln College, is a lifelong Logan County farmer.

189

*Our*Town

Exchanging VOWS

Former Sister Martha finds new life that includes husband, but she still does God's work

Poverty and obedience weren't the tough ones. In the end it was the vow of chastity and the resulting loneliness that drove Sister Martha to break her solemn oath.

"When I said I was going to be a nun forever, I meant it with every particle of my soul," she said.

Thirty-six years later, after 13 years of soul searching, Sister Martha left the Franciscan order. She left Joliet, a city her family had called home for five generations.

And she left behind a five-decade affiliation with St. Francis Academy, where she had attended high school and then served as teacher, principal and president.

Something was missing in her life. The advanced college degrees, professional achievement and camaraderie with her fellow sisters was no longer enough.

Her journey would take her from inner-city Chicago to rural downstate Lincoln where she would at last find what she was looking for.

Catholic career

Margaret Connor joined the Sisters of St. Francis Mary Immaculate in 1953. She would later adopt the name Sister Martha because she was born on the Feast of St. Martha.

It was a different era when young girls drawn to Catholic education became nuns. Though she dated and went to the prom, Margaret had no qualms about becoming a nun. It combined her love of religion, teaching and humanitarianism.

"I didn't think I'd miss men," she said. "I knew I'd miss having babies."

Her father and uncles had doubts.

"It's a tough life and my father was convinced I wasn't going to be happy," Margaret said.

Margaret pushed aside her dad's concerns and with girlish enthusiasm, she entered the convent. She said goodbye to her family and her high school

Poverty and obedience weren't the tough ones. In the end it was the vow of chastity and the resulting loneliness that drove Sister Martha to break her solemn oath.

"When I said I was going to be a nun forever, I meant it with every particle of my soul," she said.

Thirty-six years later, after 13 years of soul searching, Sister Martha left the Franciscan order. She left Joliet, a city her family had called home for five generations.

And she left behind a five-decade affiliation with St. Francis Academy, where she had attended high school and then served as teacher, principal and president.

Something was missing in her life. The advanced college degrees, professional achievement and camaraderie with her fellow sisters was no longer enough.

Her journey would take her from inner-city Chicago to rural downstate Lincoln where she would at last find what she was looking for.

Catholic career

Margaret Connor joined the Sisters of St. Francis Mary Immaculate in 1953. She would later adopt the name Sister Martha because she was born on the Feast of St. Martha.

It was a different era when young girls drawn to Catholic education became nuns. Though she dated and went to the prom, Margaret had no qualms about becoming a nun. It combined her love of religion, teaching and humanitarianism.

"I didn't think I'd miss men," she said. "I knew I'd miss having babies."

Her father and uncles had doubts.

"It's a tough life and my father was convinced I wasn't going to be happy," Margaret said.

Margaret pushed aside her dad's concerns and with girlish enthusiasm, she entered the convent. She said goodbye to her family and her high school

WHAT IS A FARMER?

A farmer is a paradox. He is an executive in overalls with his home
his office; a scientist using fertilizer attachments, a purchasing
agent in an old straw hat; a personnel director with grease under
his fingernails; a dietician with a passion for alfalfa, aminos, and an-
tibiotics; a production expert with a surplus; a manager battling a
price-cost squeeze. He manages more capital than most business-
men in town.

He likes sunshine, good food, State Fairs, dinner at noon, auctions,
his shirt collar unbuttoned, and, above all, a good soaking rain in
August.

He likes sunshine, good food, State Fairs, dinner at noon, auctions, *The Wedding*

Farmers are found in fields plowing up, seeding down, planting to,
fertilizing with, spraying against and finally harvesting it. Wives help
them; little boys follow them. The Agriculture Department confuses
them; City relatives visit them. Salesmen detain and wait for them;
weather can delay them but it takes Heaven to stop them.

A farmer is both Faith and Fatalist. He must have Faith to continually
meet the challenges of his capacities amid an ever-present possibility that an act of God (a late spring, early frost, tornados, floods,
droughts) can bring his business to a standstill. You can reduce his
acreage, but you can't restrain his ambition.

He is not much for droughts, ditches, throughways, experts, weeds,
the eight-hour day, grasshoppers, or helping with housework.

Might as well put up with him. He is your friend, your competitor,
your customer, your source of food and fiber, and self-reliant young
citizens to help replenish your cities. He is your countryman--a
denim-dressed, business-wise, fast-growing statesman of stature.
And when he comes in at noon, having spent the energy of his
hopes and dreams, he can be recharged with the magic words:
"The market's up."

**By columnist Bud Lee, county director and farm advisor for
University of California, 1985**

*Honeymoon in
Moline, Il. with my farmer*

191

Thou art holy, Lord God, who alone workest wonders. Thou art strong. Thou art great. Thou art most high. Thou art the almighty king. Thou, holy Father, king of heaven and earth. Thou art the Lord God triune and one; all good. Thou art good, all good, highest good, Lord God living and true. Thou art charity, love. Thou art wisdom. Thou art humility. Thou art patience. Thou art security. Thou art quietude. Thou art joy and gladness. Thou art justice and temperance.

JUBILEE 2006
GO FORTH AND BEAR FRUIT
JOHN 15: 16

As an assosciate of the Sisters of St. Francis, I was invited to bring up the water and wine with Jubilarians Sr. Margaret Quinn, Sr. Clare Wand, and Sr. Margaret Duffy

Seventeen

Golden Jubilee

As a young sister making my first profession of vows in Joliet in 1956, the year 2006 seemed unimaginable. That year would be our class's 50th Jubilee of being vowed Franciscan Sisters. We would joke about the year 2006 and what we would be like at that age.

As 2006 began, the Jubilee was on my mind. I was anxious to go to the familiar ceremony. I remembered my 25th year celebration very well – the beautiful mass in St. Raymond's Cathedral, the music, the joy of community, and seeing families, friends, and former students and colleagues.

My partner in the novitiate class was Sister Mary Ann Tady, also known as Sister Cleta, who had left the convent before the first profession of vows. She was coming to Lincoln from Cleveland, and we were going to drive to Joliet together to the Jubilee.

June 2006 was also a time for my quarterly visit to Mayo to check on my non-Hodgkins lymphoma.

I read a biography of Mother Alfred Moes on the way to Mayo. She is one of my personal heroines. Mother Alfred Moes had become famous in my later years. As a woman who convinced Doctor Mayo and his sons to staff St. Mary's Hospital, which she built against all odds, so that Rochester would have a hospital.

The biography told of times when Mother Alfred was a young sister in another order and had trouble with a pastor or two. Later, she had trouble with the Archbishop of Chicago. She was always thinking bigger. In photographs she looks anything but charismatic, but she must have been.

Thou art all riches to sufficiency. Thou art beauty. Thou art meekness. Thou art protector. Thou art guardian and defender. Thou art strength. Thou art refreshment. Thou art our hope. Thou art our faith. Thou art our great sweetness. Thou art our eternal life, great and admirable Lord, God almighty, merciful Savior.

WRITINGS OF ST. FRANCIS

193

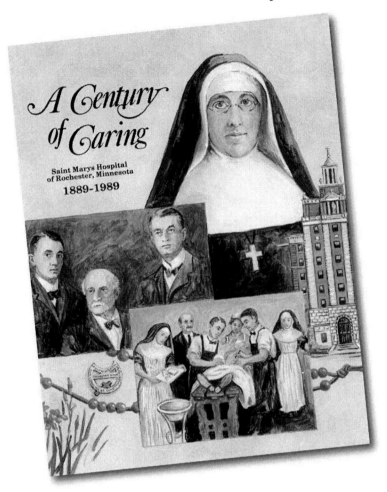

Mother Alfred began two orders of the Franciscan Sisters. The first congregation, the Sisters of St. Francis of Mary Immaculate was founded in Joliet, Illinois with Father Pamfilio. The second was the Sisters of Our Lady of Lourdes in Rochester, Minnesota. She founded the Rochester Franciscans because she was thrown out of the Chicago archdiocese, which included Joliet. The Cardinal gave her a choice to return or to stay in Rochester permanently.

My back pain was severe from low grade lymphoma, so I had to return to Mayo a second time for radiation. That meant that my visit with Mary Ann in Lincoln would be curtailed. Instead, she came early from Cleveland to drive to Mayo with me.

As Novitiate partners, Mary Ann and I lined up with each other every time we left the rooms of the Novitiate for religious services,

Golden Jubilee

Visiting the Clinic with
Jack in 2002

My heroine, Mary Alfred, co-foundress of the Mayo
Clinic, St Mary's hospital, and the Sisters of
St. Francis, Rochester, Minnesota and Joliet, Illinois

for meals, or for bed. After three years of Postulancy and Novitiate, right before first vows, Mary Ann was asked by the administration to be a cook sister. But Mary Ann wanted to teach.

The novice mistress, Sister Anacleta, called for me and told me to go to the trunk house. There on the hot second floor, I found Mary Ann crying and packing. We both were so sad.

Mary Ann is now a vowed sister in the secular institute, Our Lady of the Way. She did become a teacher and a librarian and is happy.

While Mary Ann was with me at Mayo, we visited the Rochester Franciscan motherhouse. It is a stately brick modern building on a hill overlooking the city. I was delighted to learn that the Mayo Clinic is utilizing part of the structure which was built during a time when large numbers of girls were entering the convent.

This is true for most motherhouses, or congregation centers, in the United States. There are still women who have the charism to become a sister; but they generally come in their thirties and already have a profession.

Women today do have various ways to participate in the church. The number of women who choose to serve the church and her people through a vowed life are few. But there are still a few valiant women each year who keep the charisms alive by becoming Benedictines, Dominicans, or Franciscans.

In our congregation, we have over 100 associates, similar to the Third Order to which my mom and my grandmother belonged. The associates are men, women, priests, and like me, former vowed sisters who still do their ministry in the spirit of the Joliet Franciscans. I became an associate in 2002.

The church is taking new directions, but I feel that the vowed religious commitment will always be alive and needed in the church.

Collaboration of Care
A Health and Wellness Center initiative by the University of St. Francis

The new Health and Wellness Center will be nurse-managed and offer care to some 2,550 people annually. While three populations are targeted—school children, senior citizens and domestic violence victims—the center will welcome other clients.

The main center is planned in the historic Motherhouse on the University of St. Francis' main campus. Health services will be offered to the Groundwork Domestic Violence Shelter and Lamb's Fold Women's Center. A downtown Joliet site at the Housing Authority of Joliet Murphy Building, which houses senior citizens, will be open to the public.

The new Health and Wellness Center will be nurse-managed and offer care to some 2,550 people annually. While three populations are targeted—school children, senior citizens and domestic violence victims—the center will welcome other clients.

The main center is planned in the historic Motherhouse on the University of St. Francis' main campus. Health services will be offered to the Groundwork Domestic Violence Shelter and Lamb's Fold Women's Center. A downtown Joliet site at the Housing Authority of Joliet Murphy Building, which houses senior citizens, will be open to the public.

As I was thrilled that the Mayo Clinic was utilizing the halls of Mother Alfred's legacy, the motherhouse, for expansion, I was equally thrilled to learn good news about our structure at 520 Plainfield Avenue in Joliet. The University of St. Francis, under the leadership of Dr. Michael Vinciguerra is using it as a Health and Wellness Center. The announcement reads:

> *The New Health and Wellness Center will be nurse-managed and offer care to some 2,550 people annually. While three populations are targeted – school children, senior citizens, and domestic violence victims – the center will welcome other clients.*
>
> *The main center is planned in the historic motherhouse on the University of St. Francis' main campus. Health services will be offered to the Groundwork Domestic Violence Shelter and Lamb's Fold Women's Center. A downtown Joliet site at the Housing Authority of Joliet Murphy Building, which houses senior citizens, will be open to the public.*

I think that Mother Alfred and Saint Francis would be delighted.

Standing with statues of Doctor Mayo & Mother Alfred

In Rochester, Mary Ann and I took our pictures with large statues of Doctor Mayo and Mother Alfred that were located in a new park at the Mayo Clinic.

Mary Ann drove when we returned to Lincoln from Mayo. We arrived home on June 16, with a few hours to rest before we traveled to Joliet for our Jubilee the next day.

Thankfully, Jack volunteered to drive us and join the celebration. This eased the stress of the trip, and I was glad to have him with us. I thought to myself that Mother Immaculate would be proud.

With Jeanne and Betty at an Associates retreat

Former aspirants celebrating their 50th Aniversary of SFA graduation (Class of 1954)

Golden Jubilee

Cathedral of St. Raymond

We arrived at St. Raymond's Cathedral early, which was wonderful. We heard the choir rehearse. We saw an ambulance in front of the Cathedral. I learned that my dear friend, Sister Marie Grunloh, had tripped and broken her nose.

My classmate, Sister Mary Jean told me that I was included in the mass of celebration. I felt so welcomed.

Together, Sister Peggy Quinn, silver jubilarian, and I brought up the water and wine for communion. My two friends, Sister Margaret Duffy and Sister Clare Wand, as celebrants of 60 years, brought up the bread.

Jack, Mary Ann, and another classmate and associate, Betty Maloney, and I sat in the third row behind the family of our classmate, Sister Jo Anne Marusa. She was the only one with her mother present.

Because I had arrived early, I was able to greet many sisters. I was celebrating mass with my Jubilarian classmates.. I was sitting with my beloved Jack, and my dear friends. I felt jubilant.

Golden Jubilee!

Hail Mary, full of grace, the Lord is with thee. Blessed art thou among women, and blessed is the fruit of Thy womb, Jesus. Holy Mary, Mother of God, pray for us sinners, now and at the hour of our death. Amen.

A life-long friend, Sr. Mary Jean Morris, past President of the Congregation and pastor in Mississippi

My classmate, Sr. Mary Olivieri, who has a nun sister in the Notre Dame community

Classmate Sr. Joanne Marusa, with her family; she has two nephews who are priests!

Golden Jubilee

Two Mary Anns--my class-mates: Sister Mary Ann Glascott (Jubilarian) and Mary Ann Tady

Here's to 50 Years!

St. Pat's grade school class of 1949

MAGNIFICAT

My soul proclaims the greatness of the Lord, my spirit rejoices in God my Savior for he has looked with favor on his lowly servant. From this day all generations will call me blessed: the Almighty has done great things for me, and holy is his Name.

He has mercy on those who fear him in every generation. He has shown the strength of his arm, he has scattered the proud in their conceit. He has cast down the mighty from their thrones, and has lifted up the lowly.

Eighteen

Thank You Jesus, Alleluia!

Although I was in the midst of chemotherapy, when I turned 70, with Jack's help, I made it to all of my birthday parties.

My first party was with my Logan Friday night buddies. We meet every Friday night but the birthday brought out special festivities. At this party, Gail Hunter gave me a gift certificate which volunteered her to tape and type my life story. I also got a large bottle of "Sister Margarita" Mix.

I also had two 70th birthday parties in Joliet. The first was with my Academy teaching friends and the Connor family. The second was with the McCauley women.

My cousins ranged in age from two months to close to seventy-four years old. My cousin Pat's daughters, Mary Kay and Anne, hosted. Jack is good to all our visitors. Having a lovely home and a welcoming husband is one of the joys of my 70th year. We've had McCauley reunions and Peifer reunions here and smaller reunions with lifelong friends and former students.

My 70th year included many celebrations. One was the visit of my friend Ruthie from Muenster, Texas, a close childhood friend from about age nine. We were like sisters. Her daughter Christy and her son Nathan joined us for a week. I remember Ruthie sobbing the day I left for the convent.

A teaching buddy from my years at Holy Trinity, Richard Krull, and his lovely wife Mira, who also taught at Holy Trinity, came to visit with son James and daughter Deborah – two gifted children. We enjoyed reminiscing about my turbulent Holy Trinity years.

He has filled the hungry with good things, and the rich he has sent away empty. He has come to the help of his servant Israel for he has remembered his promise of mercy, the promise he made to our fathers, to Abraham and his children for ever.

LUKE 1:46-55

Tracy Connor appearing on HUFF! June 25 on Showtime

Thank
you
Jesus,
Alleluia!

Each picture
is a chapter of
my life

Rita Matichak of Joliet ROB MATTISON/SUN PUBLICATIONS

Rita Matichak of Joliet celebrates her victory in the Ms. National Senior Citizen pageant.

By Annie Alleman
STAFF WRITER

One of the answers Rita Matichak gave at the Ms. National Senior Citizen pageant was inspired by a fledgeling Joliet phenomena. During the interview portion of the competition, held on a Tuesday, she was asked the question: "Why do you feel you would make a good representative for senior citizens?"

"I said then, 'When I drive around town, I see

"I feel like I would like to aspire in my life to inspire people to do something. I feel you must age gracefully ... and try to make every moment in life count for good.' I would like to inspire people. It's part of being an optimist."

Thomas Jefferson School who have championed its message and enlisted others to do so as well.

Matichak, who just passed her 66th birthday, is "still on cloud nine," after winning the Ms. National Senior Citizen pageant at the Hemmens Cultural Center in Elgin on July 15.

"I truly didn't expect it, perhaps that's why it means so much extra to me," she said. "I was just wonderfully surprised."

While she's a beautiful, effervescent woman,

Matichak has never been the type to enter pageants. She was married to husband Andy at 19, and had five children before her 27th birthday. In fact, this was only her second pageant. She entered the contest the first time in October 1968, kind of on a whim.

"I never saw myself doing pageants, there was never an opportunity to do anything like this before, I thought. 'Why don't I just do this,'" she said. "It'll be interesting to see what it's like and to meet new people. I needed an upper anyways." Her mother died three months earlier.

She ended up taking first runner-up in the pageant. Rather than participate last year, she chose to go to Rome with a group from her church, St. Raymond's Cathedral. Instead, this year, she thought she'd try it again. It's a motto to do her best at whatever she tries, the pageant was no exception.

knew I could meet some good people and try myself. The preparations were very demanding — there's a lot of organization and planning," she said. "You arrive on a Tuesday and the final competition is on Sunday, so it's like a week of your life that you have to be willing to give up.

On Tuesday, each of the 25 contestants were interviewed. For this they score job interview attire. At each round of competition, at each stage,

✦ *Turn to* **PAGEANT, G4**

CHRISTMAS
GOSPEL

*The Lord
became flesh
and dwells
among us.*

LUKE

I love
Christmas

Thank you Jesus, Alleluia!

Jack's Cronin cousins visit VFW & Jack and Charlie in Ireland

With Mary Jo and Lynn

With Joliet friends in front of my house
Ruthie, on the right, came from Texas

Babies are a plate of joy.

—CELE BONA

Colin as Batman
and Colin with Jack

With cousin
Rachel

Ruthie's
grandson
who came
to visit me

Suzanne
as a
child

Family of Sherlyn,
my CURVES coach

Kiernan Shipka

Thank you Jesus, Alleluia!

Kiernan. Her grandmother is my cousin Rosie. Her mom, Erin, was an SFA student while I was principal

Kiernan wearing outfit from "Beans and Such" - Lincoln

My student, Kathy
Carew-Vie's family

The sweet daughters of Dr.
Amy Facinelli Stone

Baby Jack

One of the riches of being in my 70s is seeing so much of life unfold. I felt such joy when my former student Susan Bruno, a friend and fellow Franciscan got a prestigious award at Notre Dame where she is on staff. Mary Jo Burns, a woman I hired to teach religion at the Academy in the 70s, won an award at the grade school where she had been the principal for ten years. Ascension in Oak Park is now nationally acclaimed as excellent.

It is joyful having wise women friends in their 80s and 90s – Viola, Angie, Jeanette, and of course, Aunt Kate.

And I am grateful for my "domestic divas" – Rita, Ronda, Lynn, and Veronica – who keep me on keel!

Recently, I've had the joy of reconnecting with a graduate of SFA who lives in Rochester, Paula Uremovic, who is now Dr. Laskowski and a mother, bee keeper, and friend.

O God, who hast deigned to give us blessed Francis as our guide and teacher to follow in the footsteps of Thine only-begotten Son, graciously grant that we, who celebrate his memory here on earth, may become partakers of his glory in the world to come.

Collage from my friend,
Sister Sue Bruno

I love the way Gail Sheehy denotes life's passages. We have a life passage every five or ten years. She refers to the "Serene 60s," the "Sage 70s," and the "Uninhibited 80s."

I think I've started the "Uninhibited 80s" early. I do more swearing, saying "no," and kissing Jack in public.

And I don't apologize for being a Republican.

My gait is slower, my word recall is slower – but not my life.

I am blessed.

I thank God everyday for my gracious husband Jack.

One of the nicest things about being seventy is looking back and being able to say, "I got a few things right."

I'd like to write a litany of thanks – instead I'll keep journaling and trying "To read with open eyes the book my days are writing."

Thank you Jesus. Alleluia!

My niece, Tracy Connor, an
actress, writer, and comedi-
enne, has full rights to continue using my life story in
her work

212

Appendices

Martha as Mentor

by Maureen Andrews Thomas

The cover of the book reads "… an old man, a young man, and life's greatest lesson." My Morrie is eleven years my senior and our journey spans over 40 years. We have witnessed name changes, career changes, and location changes. Our relationship is fluid. It flows from teacher to student and from friend to friend. My Morrie has been my teacher in all things. She has not only taught me how live a happy, productive life, she has walked with me while I sorted it out.

Her name is Margaret Connor Peifer, but when she entered my life, she was Sister Martha, OSF, a 26-year-old, smiling, Franciscan nun. I was 15 years old and in pain. My father had just died suddenly, and Sister Martha was just too nice. I was skeptical. She seemed almost silly, overly friendly, and very accessible. She was always looking to do small acts of kindness. She was the real deal. That was her mission – to teach her students how to pursue a happy life. She did it everyday through acts of thoughtfulness. This extremely extroverted woman would not let me be.

Sister Martha was a doer, actively seeking joy in everyday life. She also demanded accomplishments of her students and wanted to stretch their minds.

Sister Martha saw more in me than I saw in myself. She introduced me to a revolutionary way of life, and her gospel was one of joy in everyday living. She would always do little things to help us and acknowledged our quest to be true to ourselves and capitalize on our talents. Always restless, and never quite getting the vow of obedience right, she pushed the limits.

Sister Martha sought out avenues to express and showcase her students' talents. Essay contests, variety shows, letters of recommendation were just small parts of the repertoire she used to help develop the potential she saw in her pupils.

She was remarkable in the classroom. Well ahead of her time, Sister Martha was innovative and vibrant. She used a variety of methods to get her message across. I have retained much of what she taught because it struck a chord. Work was not a penance, and teaching was her joy – her bliss. She was contagious!

Our teacher-to-student relationship lasted throughout my college years. We had a letter-writing friendship. I would pour out my heart

215

to her, and her advice was kind and sound. However, our relationship could not be pigeonholed into a simple mentor-to-student role. As we moved on to our next phases in life, so did our friendship.

I set out on a traditional path. I taught school, got married, and raised five children. Meanwhile, Sister Martha was going through an enormous struggle. After 30 years in the convent, she left the order and once again became Margaret Connor. She started out on her own. Always true to herself, she filled her new apartment with pictures of smiling faces to cheer up her days. Her name had changed, but the core of her the person had not. She was still on a mission to teach.

Margaret had always been a city person, but she moved on to a new adventure. Her next teaching assignment was very non-traditional. She accepted the position of Education Director of Logan Correctional Facility in rural Lincoln, Illinois. Always blooming where she is planted, Margaret set out to bring her positive philosophy to her prison work and to the local community. She got more than she bargained. She got Jack.

Margaret said of Jack Peifer, "He is as much a farmer as I am a teacher." She had met her soulmate who was a bachelor and a farmer. Almost 30 years after she attended my wedding, I was privileged to be part of her wedding celebration.

Ironically some of Margaret's greatest lessons were taught during both of our battles with cancer. In 1996, she was diagnosed with lymphoma. During her illness, she was the master communicator in our relationship. She kept me informed of her condition and assured all that she would make it. Four years later, it was my turn to battle cancer, and Margaret bombarded me with expressions of love and care. Phone calls, flowers, candles, and cards with notes were sent to strengthen my resolve. A particularly bittersweet gift was that of a beautiful straw hat to cover my not-so-beautiful bald head. We conversed regularly about our cancer wars. Once again, Margaret was there to lead the way.

Recently, Margaret and Jack joined my family to celebrate our 35th wedding anniversary. It was a time to reflect on the many blessings in life, and one of life's greatest is Margaret Connor-Peifer. I still picture her as she was in 1962. My mind shoots back to the needy 15-year-old, and my heart remembers with sincere gratitude the wisdom and kindness of that 26 year old nun.

Margaret and Lincoln

By Nancy Rollings Saul

I don't exactly remember the first time I met Margaret Connor. It was probably the autumn of 1993, when she started laying groundwork for a historical marker for internationally acclaimed black poet, Langston Hughes.

I wasn't familiar with Hughes or his work, but I was swept along with a host of other people on the wave of Margaret's enthusiasm.

That was about a year after Margaret was named education administrator for Logan Correctional Center and moved to Lincoln from Chicago, where she had been working. In 1993, she planned an in-service training program for her teaching staff at Logan.

During the local history presentation, Paul Gleason mentioned that Langston Hughes had lived in Lincoln as a youngster and wrote his first poem there. Gleason said Hughes inscribed copies of three of his published books to his eighth-grade teacher, Ethel Welch. The inscribed books are owned by Lincoln Community High School.

By Margaret's own admission she went nuts.

"I had been teaching Hughes' poems in my English classes for years," she said.

There was no way she could rest until a plaque dedicated to Hughes was erected somewhere in Lincoln, but first, she had to educate the public. Margaret contacted Russell Allen at the Lincoln Public Library to verify Hughes' Central School attendance. Then she helped plan a spring 1994 library display. Hughes was born in February, so he fit nicely into Black History Month.

With cajoling from Margaret, Ann Klose and I put together a story with photos and some of Hughes' poems for a mid-February LifeStyle feature in *The Courier*.

Then the project faded from public eye until February 1995. That's when Margaret imported Dr. Marcellus Leonard, an acclaimed Springfield poet, to do a reading for the Hughes project. This event was to be a fundraiser as well as an educational venue.

I put together two folders. Each had a copy of Hughes' poem, "Dreams," and a tiny sterling bird to illustrate the poem. We presented one to Leonard and offered the second for auction.

When no one bid on the item, Margaret reached into her own pocket and bid the exact amount we hoped the piece would bring.

I felt so bad that she had to do that, so the next day, I donated an equal amount to the Hughes project. The fundraiser had some success, even though the contributors were limited.

At the Third Annual Hughes Celebration, in 1996, fundraising began in earnest. That year, the celebration featured Joe Hackett's students from Central School reading excerpts of Hughes' poems.

That autumn, a second fundraiser was held at Abe's Carmelcorn and Prairie Years bookstore. By that time, the Friends of Langston Committee had more than 50 members.

On December 7, 1996, the committee presented 1,250 dollars to the Illinois State Historical Society for a Hughes commemorative plaque. Abraham Lincoln Tourism Bureau of Logan County pledged 300 dollars

In October 1998, Hughes' plaque was dedicated on a corner near the School. The building has been replaced, but the plaque remains.

The Hughes project took five years, and the final 600 dollars in expenses wasn't paid to the historical society until the year the marker was erected. Margaret never lost faith that the costs would eventually be paid. During those five years, we became better acquainted through her publicity-seeking trips to *The Courier*, and both belonged to Holy Family Catholic Church.

I learned that she has been an educator her whole professional life, adding administrative duties as she gained experience. I also learned that she was a former nun, and that intrigued me.

As a cradle Methodist who didn't convert to Catholicism until my 30s, I had never known a nun before, let alone a former nun. I wasn't sure quite what to make of her. It didn't take me long to figure out that she was still very connected to the church.

I figured she had the answers to some of those theological mysteries and Catholic peculiarities with which I still struggled.

Once after we attended a meeting where the subject of church attendance was discussed, she told me, "Sometimes when people ask me about a good church to attend, I send them somewhere else."

"I just don't think the Catholic church is very friendly. I am sustained by the Eucharist, but if they're looking for someplace warm and welcoming, I send them elsewhere."

I don't think I gasped, but I must have looked startled. She told me how difficult it had been for her to leave the convent after promising to be a nun forever. The leave-taking process took her 13 years.

She said, "I had a sense of failure, but the Lord only gave me one life, and I had to move on. I felt lonely. I didn't know much about money or men. Suddenly, I was Margaret Connor, and I didn't know who Margaret Connor was. I'd never been Margaret Connor."

She rented an apartment in Chicago, where she was working.

"The living room looked too big," she said.

For years, her personal space had consisted of a small bedroom, known as a cell, at the convents where she was assigned. She shared the public spaces with other members of her order.

"I took a bedroom and put pictures of smiling faces and my TV in it," she said. "I made it like a little womb."

With her characteristic enthusiasm, she also signed up for a computer dating service. I really don't know what I expected from former nuns in the romance department, but somehow, this surprised me. Although she had plenty of other credentials and attractive attributes, I wondered if she added "former nun" to her profile.

Margaret and Lincoln

"Having left the convent at age 57, I wanted to find a companion, a husband, and I wanted to do this quickly," she said. Then added, "I'm not sure which I was more naive about, relationships or money."

She dated several men that summer but didn't find anyone special.

During the Hughes project, other areas of Margaret's life were unfolding. She was diagnosed with cancer and began treatment. However, she was so distraught that a beloved nephew was dying of cancer that her own illness became almost secondary to her.

Her nephew was handsome, talented, and a recent college graduate with had a beautiful girlfriend.

I met Margaret at a local restaurant one evening to discuss a project with her, but she told me tearfully that she wouldn't be able to concentrate on that until she told me about his death, which was a great blow to her.

But happier events were afoot. One day, Margaret dropped a news release on my desk. As she turned to walk out of the office, she mentioned in a very low-key way, "Oh, I'm engaged now." Old stereotypes die hard – former nun, nearly 60 – I thought I misunderstood her. I saw her a few more times, and she never mentioned it again. I wasn't sure it would be polite to ask, so I didn't.

But one day, Margaret came by the office again. This time, she was flashing a beautiful diamond solitaire and announced that she was going to marry Jack Peifer.

"Jack has all of these relatives who are in the convent," she said. "He understands and appreciates me."

In fact, Jack Peifer is the nephew of Margaret's first superior at the Joliet convent, Mother Immaculate Buckstegge. By divine intervention, he and his mother lived on a farm just outside of Lincoln.

On February 16, 1998, Jack and Margaret's family and friends packed Holy Family Catholic Church for a joyous wedding. It was a first marriage for both of them.

"Margaret," explained one of the presiding priests, "has always had a restless heart - seeking more - giving more - she has enlightened and brightened so many of our lives and stretched us with her restless yearning for more."

After the wedding, Margaret struggled with *The Courier's* wedding announcement form. She finally decided to shorten her considerable educational achievements to a couple of degrees to accomodate the space on the form.

"I couldn't have children," she said, obviously embarrassed, "so I pursued degrees."

The Peifers built a cozy cottage on the farm. Margaret finally retired from the correctional center but not from teaching. She can never resist the lure of one more opportunity to teach.

Following the Hughes project, Margaret helped get a plaque erected to honor theologian Gustav Niebuhr, author of "The Serenity Prayer." The prayer is often used by 12-step recovery programs.

Another such plaque followed to honor former New Yorker editor William Maxwell, who wrote several stories based on his early years in Lincoln, Illinois, and again, Margaret assisted its creation.

As a member of the board, she shows up annually before the fundraiser for Catholic Social Services. She's very willing to help people dispose of pieces of art that no longer fit their decor.

She also remained close to our family. When my daughter was considering a religious vocation, I sent her to talk with Margaret.

She and Margaret have remained special friends through her years at Franciscan University at Steubenville and through her decision to serve the church through marriage and family. One year, the Peifers even used an image of my daughter bathing her firstborn on their Christmas cards.

For three years, Margaret has nominated a local educator for *The Courier's* Citizen of the Year award. Her candidate hasn't yet been picked from among the many nominees, but she's probably sharpening her pencil for the next round.

You see, Margaret is determined, generous to a fault, brave in the face of recurring cancer, loyal, and loving to her many friends.

Wedding Homily

Fr. Bob Colaresi, O'Carm

**Margaret (Martha) Conner - John Peifer
16 February 1998**

Jack finally smiled!

Hearing 1st reading by Tracy - reason to be nervous
- "good wife puts flesh on his bones!"
- "governed speech" - Margaret???
* good wife - "live twice as long!!!"*

It is an ethnic stereotype, rooted in reality, that the Irish marry later in life - but this marriage is stretching and expanding that stereotype.

Charlie 40 - she is 62 - average marrying age: 51 - what example does this set for the Connor children!!

Many of us have walked with Jack and Margaret - and are thrilled that this day has come ! I've watched and listened to Margaret's restless search for many years, and I'm happy to see her so happy!

Speaking of Margaret, whom I know best, this is also another nominal transition for us - she was born and baptized Margaret, even though she was born on the feast of St. Martha - then following a call, she became Sr. Martha - most of us simply called her Martha, and like the biblical one, she was banging pops and pans in the experience of our lives. Her family and childhood friends knew her as Muggs or Muggsy - then, as her journey continued, she seemed to be reverting - she became her baptismal Margaret again - that nominal transition was difficult for many of us, so we baptized her - Margatha -

1

which covered her both ways. And now she is Mrs. Jack Peifer. More names than most of us have jobs!

I presume that Jack has been Jack, has been Jack!

We should be just and fair! I understand that some of Jack's old, (opps former!) girlfriends are here, and maybe we should get them up here to tell their story. There may be more to this quiet man than seems obvious.

We are here to celebrate with you and for you, Jack and Margaret - we are happy for you - it is refreshing that in the golden years of your lives you still seek the springtime - of new hope, new life - richer life of promise. It is exciting that life has not made you two cynical nor suspicious - afraid to take the risk of love and commitment - that you still dream - the ancient dream echoed in the first reading you chose from the Book of Sirach, which Tracy read for us - the blessing a husband and wife are to each other - that your commitment and love, refined by life's experience, is like the sun rising in the Lord's heaven - it is another springtime - and time of light - for you - and for us!

We know you two to be people rooted in God and our Catholic faith - God and the community of faith are important parts of your lives. It is interesting that you have not chosen to simply remain friends - close, good friends and companions - you could have easily raced your rocking chairs into the sunset separately, on parallel paths. It is rare, if not unprecedented, to have two people in their 60s getting married - and it being their first marriage for both. But you have been called and have chosen to be married and enter into the Sacrament of

2

Marriage in the Roman Catholic tradition. The reality, call and work of God within you two is obvious here.

In the second reading from Colossians, which Tom proclaimed for us, we hear the heart of love - the heart of your commitment - to love, cherish, forgive, honor, reverence and serve, united in thanksgiving and life - the way God loves us in Christ - the way the Spirit of Jesus breathes and works among us - the way you, Margaret and Jack are committed to be for each other. It is good - it is wholesome - it is life-giving, humbling and awesome - it is holy! It is of God - and it is yours!

There is something strange and wonderful about the way God works - there is almost something incestuous about Margaret and Jack - at least religious incest. We all know that Margaret was Sr. Martha for many years - a Joliet Franciscan sister. It is interesting that, besides Fr. Claude, Jack's family has so many Nuns in it - at least four that I'm aware of - and two were Joliet Franciscans - ala Sr. Martha - and his Aunt, Mother Immaculate was even the Mother General of the Joliet Franciscans and Sr. Martha's first superior as a young Nun. The God of history has a wonderful sense of humor and way of bringing everything together - even if it looks incestuous. Jack, even as you gain a wonderful woman as your wife, there is also another Nun in your family. I'm sure that Mother Immaculate is smiling down saying: "Margaret and Jack, I always knew!"

Besides a strong Roman Catholicism and Nundom, Jack and Margaret share a lot of interests, like dancing - wholehearted dedication to who they are and what they do. Margaret explained: "Jack is as much of a farmer as I am

3

an educator" - and that is thorough, deep and complete dedication. They both love people and being around people, but do it in very different ways.

The wonderful Gospel of the Beatitudes, which they chose, says so much about them and the ways God is working within and through them. The images of Salt and Light are wonderful - they are metaphors we don't put together well in life or poetry. But Jesus did - and so do Margaret and Jack. The obvious image of Jack as a farmer - "salt of the earth" comes to mind. Salt is the ancient preservative - it adds taste, richness of flavor, depth - just as farmers make God's earth productive - they dig, unearth, plant, fertilize, water, patiently tend and weed, allowing roots to sink deep, and life to blossom. Farmers have the rhythm of God's earth in their souls - and it salts and softens the human experience with depth, life, patience and wisdom. Jack is certainly a prime example of being "salt of the earth" in the best sense that Jesus meant it. He comes from a long tradition of this earth and this Church - his family have been active participants here for 150 years. Life blossoms from great depth with that kind of rootedness!

Light is an obvious image for Margaret - the Teacher in her enlightens, with passion and conviction - she is enthusiastic - effusive - she radiates life - light is energy defused - it is effusive in an elusive way - it makes things clearer and brighter - it also creates shadows which give depth and texture to things. If farmers are about roots, light is about wings - and Margaret is certainly someone who lives on the wings of dreams and seeks the more. She has always had a restless heart - seeking more - giving

4

more - she has enlightened and brightened so many of our lives - and stretched us with her restless yearning for more. I've tried - she is not a light that can be easily hidden under a bushel basket - she is an energizer bunny who springs to life and always makes resurrection happen. Life is always more fun and brighter when Margaret is light present. She has faced the painful shadows in her own life and her family and friends - and her fire, energy and passion has only become brighter. She loves people - and we have all shined brighter because of her love and footsteps in our lives.

(story of Naperville parish - trouble she caused me! - she brings lots of life and light - but also trouble!!)

Yet, the more you look at Margaret and Jack, as opposite and different as they are, the light and salt imagery applies to both of them. Light is about creating life - farmers dig deep that life can blossom and share the light of day - plants spread their winged leaves and flowers to grow - and feed others - in self-giving that it eternal light. Jack is the quiet lighthouse, always glowing in the darkness, guiding to safe shores. Faithful light deepens and comforts the human experience.

And Margaret is salty - she adds flavor, spice and sparkle - she brings out the best in things and people - she preserves and digs deep - there is always more with Margaret which needs to be touched, enriched, enhanced, explored.

They are both salt and light - and through them God helps create and brighten the human experience. We are

5

thrilled that you are together - that you are so different and complementary. Life will be deeper and brighter for you - and for us!

God has called you into the Sacrament of Marriage, because the Holy One, Our God needs and wants you to tell the world how much, how deeply, and how enthusiastically He loves us. People will know the depth, feel and enthusiasm of God's love for them by seeing and experiencing how much you two love and are life-giving each other. This is what the Sacrament of Marriage means in our Roman Catholic tradition. You image God in your relationship with each other.

You image the God who digs deep into the human experience to plant his Word and to embrace our hearts, giving us comfort, depth and stability. You image the God who is the leaven of the human experience, expanding us on the wings of the Spirit of Jesus that God's Kingdom might blossom.

Farmer - Teacher, Salt and Light - Wings and Roots - Lover and Beloved - Margaret and Jack, thank you for accepting this call and responsibility.

You both love to dance - and as we celebrate your wedding and wish you the best, we pray that the image you project to each other and to us - is the eternal message of God - and now your sacramental mission and life: "May I have this dance for the rest of my life!!!"

Congratulations Margaret and Jack! We love you! We bless you!

6

Peifer Reflection

by Abbott Claude Peifer

REFLECTIONS FOR THE MARRIAGE OF JACK PEIFER AND MARGARET CONNOR
FEBRUARY 16, 1998

For a long time now the principal occasion for my participating in family gatherings has been to celebrate funerals. Over the years I have been at enough of them that I think I may have at least one of the qualifications necessary to run for vice-president. Consequently it is a special joy to be here today for a very different kind of celebration. Like everyone else here today, I am grateful to Margaret and Jack for the opportunity to celebrate their wedding with them, and to pray with this whole assembly for God's blessing upon their life together.

You do not need another homily at this point. I have been asked, however, to offer a meditation, so I propose to follow Margaret's suggestion—as everyone seems to do—that I might reflect upon the long relationship of the Peifer family to this parish community.

I am a second cousin of Jack. His father, Henry, and my father, John, were first cousins. His grandfather, Frank, and my grandfather, John, were brothers. John was the third oldest and Frank the second youngest of a family of nine children; they were eight years apart. Both were the sons of our common ancestor, Nicholas.

Nicholas Peifer was born in the Moselle Valley four years after the battle of Waterloo. In 1847, when he was 28 years old, he emigrated to the United States, where he was eventually followed by his younger brother and four sisters. His coming to Illinois is probably explained by its reputation for being a good place for farming, in which he had had experience at home.

At first he worked in the Chicago area, and I am not sure in what year he came to Springfield, but I believe he was working in Sangamon County at least by 1850. Two years later, in Springfield, he married a lady named Katherine Roach, who had recently arrived from County Galway in Ireland by way of New Orleans—the beginning of a pattern of marrying Irish wives that seems not yet to have run its course.

What was central Illinois like in 1850? We do not know whether Nicholas ever had occasion to meet a fellow citizen of Springfield named Abraham Lincoln, ten years older than he. Eventually he would settle in a town named for this man, and the two decades that Nicholas spent in Illinois before he came here were dominated by momentous issues and events that are forever associated with Lincoln's name: the spread of slavery to new territories such as Nebraska and Kansas, and the terrible civil war that was eventually fought to settle this question.

The prairie was still untouched in many places, and in 1854 Nicholas was able to buy his own farm, 80 acres of open prairie in Tazewell County. The family lived there for the next thirteen years, near the present town of Armington, and six of their children were born there. They farmed and raised hogs, which had to be loaded on sleds in the winter and taken to market in Pekin. In 1867 they sold this place and made their final move, to a farm in Logan County, eight miles northeast of Lincoln, in East Lincoln Township, where Nicholas acquired 160 acres.

Both Nicholas and Katherine brought their Catholic faith with them from their respective homelands, but they found very different religious conditions here. In Illinois they came into the new diocese of Chicago, created only a few years earlier, in 1843, and embracing the entire state, which had previously been divided between St. Louis and Vincennes. It was not until 1877 that they became part of a new diocese centered in Peoria.

However, it was easier to create dioceses than it was to staff them. Until the railroads were built through Illinois in the 1850's, Catholics were served mostly by traveling priests who made their way from one settlement to another on horseback or by river boat. The first Catholic parish in Springfield, now the cathedral, dates from 1839, but the Catholics there were unable to build even a very modest church building until 1848. Nicholas must have found this church just completed when he arrived, and presumably he and Katherine first worshiped there. In Tazewell County it could not have been easy, and probably was often impossible, to attend Mass. The closest places would have been Bloomington, where the first parish began in 1853, or Pekin, where a parish had been established in 1841. But in the decade before the civil war the new railroads brought in thousands of new settlers, so that the population exploded, and priests came, mostly from Europe, to shepherd them.

Lincoln was incorporated as a city in 1853, and four years later a resident priest arrived and began St. Patrick's Parish for the mostly Irish Catholics. When Nicholas and his family came here to stay in 1867, the parish had already been established for ten years. They remained members of this local church for the rest of their lives and are buried here, in Holy Cross Cemetery. Many of their descendants, to the fourth generation, have followed in their footsteps to the present day, 130 years later.

At this point the question arises, How did all these Germans end up in an Irish parish? Part of the answer is, of course, that in 1867 they didn't have any choice. But ten years later the German Catholics in Lincoln obtained their own parish, one block away on Fourth Street. However, the Peifers stayed where they were. The explanation for this, I think, comes back to the Irish women. It was the custom (indeed, the law, I think) that marriages took place in the parish of the bride, and the resulting families afterwards remained there. Thus the Peifers married themselves into Irish parishes. Nicholas's sons married women with names like Margaret Mahoney, Mary Ryan, Elizabeth Casey, and Margaret Gabbett. So the prospect of another Irish Margaret holds no terror for us.

In the next generation, both Jack's father and mine married German wives, so our families escaped from the Irish influence and worshiped a block up the street. We were the smaller of the two congregations. I am not sure about Jack's experience, but I spent a good part of my youth keeping a lonely vigil out in right field while our softball team was being trounced by the tougher kids from the Irish school. Eventually the two schools were combined into one new one, and then, some years later, an act of God brought about the combination of the parishes as well. I have never heard any rumors or suspicions about the work of Irish arsonists, so in retrospect perhaps we can plausibly conclude that the Lord wanted to bring us all together again.

If these rambling reflections have anything serious to say about today's celebration, it is precisely this, that the Lord does want to bring us all together into one body. "For in one Spirit we were all baptized into one body, whether Jews or Greeks, slaves or free persons, and we were all given to drink of one Spirit" (1 Cor 12,13). Consequently, "there is neither Jew nor Greek, there is neither slave nor free person, there is not male and female; for you are all one in Christ Jesus" (Gal 3,28). "One Lord, one faith, one baptism, one God and Father of all" (Eph 4,5).

The Old Testament made much of the origins and history of God's people, and told at length of the search for wives for Isaac and Jacob. The continuity and fidelity of the family of Abraham and the people descended from him were the means God had chosen to bring salvation to us all. Now, since Pentecost, the Spirit has been poured forth upon all without distinction. The community of marriage and family is the most basic unit of human community, and that is why the New Testament can speak of the marriage bond as the image of the Church: "This is a great mystery, but I speak in reference to Christ and the Church" (Eph 5,32).

May the marriage of Margaret and Jack bring God's abundant blessing upon them, upon their families, and upon this local church so long entwined with our history.

Fr. Claude Peifer, O.S.B.
February 16, 1998

Books by Langston Hughes

Poetry

The Panther and the Lash (1967)
Ask Your Mama (1961)
Selected Poems of Langston Hughes (1958)
Montage of a Dream Deferred (1951)
One-Way Ticket (1949)
Fields of Wonder (1947)
Shakespeare in Harlem (1942)
The Dream-Keeper (1932)
Fine Cloths to the Jew (1927)
The Weary Blues (1926)

Fiction

Five Plays by Langston Hughes (1963)
Something in Common and Other Stories (1963)
The Sweet Flypaper of Life (1955)
Laughing to Keep from Crying (1952)
The Ways of White Folks (1934)
Not Without Laughter (1930)

Humor

Simple's Uncle Sam (1965)
Best of Simple (1961)
Simple Stakes a Claim (1957)
Simple Takes a Wife (1953)
Simple Speaks His Mind (1950)

For Young People

First Book of Africa (1964)
The First Book of the West Indies (1956)
The First Book of Rhythms (1954)
The First Book of Jazz (1954)
The First Book of Negroes (1952)
   -   with Arna Bontemps
Popo and Fifina (1932)

Bibliography & Autobiography

Famous Negro Heroes of America (1958)
I Wonder As I Wander (1956)
Famous Negro Music-Makers (1955)
Famous American Negroes (1954)
*The Big Sea (1940)

Anthology

The Langston Hughes Reader (1958)

History

   -   with Milton Meltzer
Black Magic: A Pictorial History of the Negro in American Entertainment (1967)
Fight For Freedom: The Story of the NAACP (1962)
A Pictorial History of the Negro in America (1956)

Gathered by Nancy Saul for The Lincoln Courier (2/16/94)

*   The autobiography in which Langston tells of Lincoln Central School, Ethel
Welch, and being the 8th grade class poet. He wrote to Ethel Welch for 50 years.

Langston Hughes Historical Marker

FIRST POEM BY LANGSTON HUGHES

This internationally known African-American author (1902-1967) acknowledges in his autobiography *The Big Sea* that he wrote his first poem while attending Central School here in Lincoln. Ethel Welch, his eighth grade teacher, asked him to write the graduation poem. With no experience, Hughes prepared an eight-verse piece to honor each of the school's eight instructors. And the poem was printed in the commencement program. He graduated in 1916 with a class of eighty students. Hughes, a native of Joplin, Missouri, who had grown up in Lawrence, Kansas, had come to Lincoln in 1915 to live with his mother and step-father. He attended high school in Cleveland, Ohio.

Hughes' prominence in American literature comes mainly from his poems and novels written during the Harlem Renaissance of the 1920s. His subsequent poetry, short stories, and other works, which appeared in the *Chicago Defender* and the *New York Post*, assured his fame. His literary works celebrate the African-American experience in the United States and his many admirers have bestowed on him the title of Poet Laureate of Black America. One of his most famous poems follows:

DREAMS

Hold fast to dreams
For if dreams die
Life is a broken winged bird
That cannot fly.

Hold fast to dreams
For when dreams go
Life is a barren field
Frozen with snow.

Erected by the Friends of Langston Hughes,
the Abraham Lincoln Tourism Bureau of Logan County,
and the Illinois State Historical Society, 1998.

With the permission of the estate of Langston Hughes

Langston Hughes Historical Marker

Langston
Hughes
Historical
Marker

Margaret Peifer poses with the Langston Hughes plaque
that will be unveiled Sunday near Central School.

Brief History of Langston Project

August 1991	Irene Gulup donates the three books to Lincoln Community High School. They are inscribed to Ethel Welch from Langston Hughes.
September 1993	Paul Gleason speaks at Logan Correctional Center for a teacher in-service. Committee is initiated by Ida and Henry Johnson and Margaret Connor.
January 1994	Russell Allen verifies Langston Hughes' Central School attendance through *Courier* file.
February 1, 1994	Library Display on Langston Hughes
February 16, 1994	Nancy Saul and Ann Klose feature Langston Hughes in Lifestyles section on Lincoln *Courier*
February 1, 1995	Lincoln College – Presentation – Second Annual Celebration. Dr. Marcellus Leonard featured.
February 1, 1996	Third Annual Celebration of Langston – Lincoln Public Library. Joe Hackett and students featured. Financial appeal begins.
September 15, 1996	Fundraiser at Abe's Carmelcorn and Prairie Years.
December 7, 1996	Check for $1,250.00 presented to Illinois State Historical Society. Tourism Board pledges $300.
October 18, 1998	Dedication of Marker – Central School.
December 31, 1998	Final $600 due to Illinois State Historical Society.

Lincoln to honor poet

The huge plaque, stored in Jack and Margaret Peifer's rural Lincoln garage, has been five years in the making.

Nationally acclaimed poet Langston Hughes wrote his first poem during the year he lived in Lincoln and attended Central School. The marker, made to recognize the former pupil, will be unveiled near Central during public ceremonies at 2 p.m. Sunday.

Margaret Peifer was the moving force behind the accolade.

"I'm not sure when I first fell in love with Langston, but I do remember the first scream of delight," she wrote in an assignment for an essay class.

In 1993, Peifer had planned an in-service training program for her teaching staff at Logan Correctional Center and she decided to include a segment about local history.

"And Langston Hughes wrote his first poem here in Lincoln," mentioned historian Paul Gleason during his presentation.

Sunday, Peifer will welcome those gathered near Central School to dedicate the new plaque.

new boy in the class — and black at that — connecting with his teacher that touched my heart," she wrote. "To me, discovering a talent in a person is at the heart of teaching.

"Maybe that was the attraction. For 20 years, I had attempted to inspire young people to write and appreciate writing — and never had anyone inscribed a published work to me."

Her enthusiasm also was fueled by the discovery that three signed copies of Hughes' books, inscribed to Welch, are owned by Lincoln Community High School.

Langston Hughes Historical Marker

The huge plaque, stored in Jack and Margaret Peifer's rural Lincoln garage, has been five years in the making.

Nationally acclaimed poet Langston Hughes wrote his first poem during the year he lived in Lincoln and attended Central School. The marker, made to recognize the former pupil, will be unveiled near Central during public ceremonies at 2 p.m. Sunday.

Margaret Peifer was the moving force behind the accolade.

"I'm not sure when I first fell in love with Langston, but I do remember the first scream of delight," she wrote in an assignment for an essay class.

In 1993, Peifer had planned an in-service training program for her teaching staff at Logan Correctional Center and she decided to include a segment about local history.

"And Langston Hughes wrote his first poem here in Lincoln," mentioned historian Paul Gleason during his presentation.

"I went nuts," wrote Peifer, who had been teaching Hughes' poems in her English classes for years.

She learned that Hughes made reference to this first literary attempt in his autobiography, "The Big Sea." He also mentioned his favorite teacher, Ethel Welch.

And for Peifer, ever the educator, that was the crowning touch.

"It may have been my picturing this

Sunday, Peifer will welcome those gathered near Central School to dedicate the new plaque.

new boy in the class — and black at that — connecting with his teacher that touched my heart," she wrote. "To me, discovering a talent in a person is at the heart of teaching.

"Maybe that was the attraction. For 20 years, I had attempted to inspire young people to write and appreciate writing — and never had anyone inscribed a published work to me."

Her enthusiasm also was fueled by the discovery that three signed copies of Hughes' books, inscribed to Welch, are owned by Lincoln Community High School.

"No one seems to know who donated them," Peifer said. "I wish we could find out where they came from.

"I kept picturing this spinster English teacher, receiving books from her pupil for the next 30 years. I wondered if she would excitedly share this with her neighbors and friends, or if she was a quiet, private person."

Typically, when Peifer becomes excited about an issue, she does more than muse over it, and this was no exception.

She formed a committee, made up of

233

Logan chaplain Henry Johnson, Richard Sumrall, head librarian at Lincoln Public Library, and others. Her goal was the erection of a plaque to honor Hughes.

The committee planned readings of Hughes' poetry and other events to raise funds for the marker.

"The more I read about Langston, the more I was amazed at him," Peifer wrote. "He never stopped writing and he would write anything — history, short stores, a movie, comical essays and even an opera."

Sunday, Peifer will welcome those gathered near Central School to dedicate the new plaque. Lincoln Mayor Joan Ritter and Judy Funderburg, LCHS librarian, will speak, as will a representative of the Illinois State Historical Society.

Maria Mootry teaches a class on Langston Hughes at the University of Illinois at Springfield. Sunday, the professor will read a poem she wrote about researching Hughes in Lincoln.

Members of Joe Hackett's sixth grade class at Central will perform a selection of Hughes' works. Following the unveiling of the plaque, and a song by Debbie Ross, Henry Johnson will give the benediction.

Music will be provided before and after the ceremony by the Lincoln Junior High School Jazz Band.

The new plaque reads, in part,

'Hughes' prominence in American Literature comes mainly from his poems and novels written during the Harlem Renaissance of the 1920s. His subsequent poetry, short stories and other works, which appeared in The Chicago Defender and the New York Post, assured his fame. His literary works cel-

ebrate the African American experience in the United States and his many admirers have bestowed on him the title of Poet Laureate of Black America."

"It will stand as a marker for Langston Hughes and for two idealistic English teachers," Peifer says.

"Ethel Welch and me."

Reinhold Niebuhr Historical Marker

A DEDICATION SERVICE FOR
AN ILLINOIS STATE HISTORICAL MARKER
IN HONOR OF THE NIEBUHR FAMILY

The Text of the Niebuhr Historical Marker
The Niebuhr Family of Theologians

The Niebuhr family, called "The Trapp Family of Theology" by *Time* magazine, produced four distinguished professors of Christian studies. In 1902, the Rev. Gustav and Lydia Niebuhr came to Lincoln, where he became pastor of St. John's Evangelical Church and Deaconess Hospital Administrator. All four of their children - Hulda, Walter, Reinhold, and Helmut Richard - were confirmed here.

After Gustav's death, Reinhold (1892-1971) assumed the Interim Pastorate and was ordained at St. John's on June 29, 1913. From a Detroit pastorate he moved to New York in 1928 and taught at Union Theological Seminary, exerting wide influence in religion and politics through his doctrine of Christian Realism. His works include the Serenity Prayer, used by the military, AA and other personal recovery programs. In 1948 he appeared on the cover of *Time* magazine and in 1964 he received the Presidential Medal of Freedom.

The Serenity Prayer

Lord, grant me the serenity to accept the things I cannot change, Courage to change the things I can, And the wisdon to know the difference.

Living one day at a time; Enjoying one moment at a time; Accepting hardship as the pathway to peace.

Taking, as He did, this sinful world as it is, Not as I would have it. Trusting that He will make all things right if I surrender to His will;

That I may be reasonable happy in this life, and supremeley happy with Him forever in the next. Amen.

REINHOLD
NIEBUHR

235

A DEDICATION SERVICE FOR AN ILLINOIS STATE
HISTORICAL MARKER IN HONOR OF THE NIEBUHR FAMILY

St. John United Church of Christ   2:00 p.m., Saturday, June 23, 2001

Prelude	*Prelude and Fugue in C Major by Bach*	Rachel Hall
Presentation of Colors		Boy Scout Troop 6
Solo	*America The Beautiful*	Debbie Ross
Call to Prayer		The Rev. James Cravens
Welcome		The Rev. Richard Reinwald
Introductions		Lynn Spellman
History of "Friends"		Chaplain Henry Johnson
Greetings: City of Lincoln		Mayor Beth Davis
	Lincoln Elementary School District 27	Dr. Robert Kidd, Superintendent
	Abraham Lincoln Tourism Bureau of Logan Co.	Thressia Usherwood
Illinois State Historical Society		Tom Teague
Commentary		Gustav Niebuhr
Solo	*Faith of Our Fathers*	Joye Anderson
Selected Readings		Children from Central School under the direction of Joe Hackett
Presentation of Niebuhr Marker		The Rev. Laurie Tockey
Benediction		The Rev. Richard Reinwald
Postlude	*Toccata in F Major by Buxtehude*	Rachel Hall

H. Richard Niebuhr (1894-1962), an authority on theological ethics and Church history, was President of Elmhurst College and taught at Eden Seminary in St. Louis and at Yale for 31 years. His son, Richard R. Niebuhr, taught Theology at Harvard from 1956 to 1999. Hulda Niebuhr (1889-1959) taught at Boston University and at McCormick Seminary, Chicago. Lydia's sister, Adele Hosto, was consecrated at Deaconess at St. John's in 1914 and served in Lincoln beginning in 1942.

During the Niebuhr pastorate, St. John's Evangelical Church stood at Fifth and Union Streets. St. John United Church of Christ is that church's descendant. H. Richard Niebuhr spoke at its dedication in 1925. Gustav, Lydia and Hulda Niebuhr and Adele Hosto are buried in Union Cemetery in Lincoln.

Erected by St. John United Church of Christ, Friends of the Niebuhrs, and the Illinois State Historical Society, 2001.

Thank you Jesus Collages

Pat, Pete, and sons

"Everything is Grace"

— ST. THERESE OF LISIEUX

My mentor
Margaret

Vintage friends
Mary and Paul

Staff at Logan

With John & Colin

Ali

Luke & Luke

Libby bequeaths Aunt Marian to me

Lord bless

Madeline

Ben

Colin

Thy Children

Thank
You
Jesus
Collages

Maureen & grandson

Jack & Tina

Graduation picture
with Stephen

Cindi (center) with
family & friends

So many
things for
which to be
thankful...

Colin
& Jack

St. Francis
on my patio

With my godson, Brendan

242

Collage of
Good Cheer

*Thank
You
Jesus
Collages*

Marlene
visits me in
Lincoln

Deb
adds
wine to
the roast

Ann
explains
pie
making

Tai Chi with SFA Friends

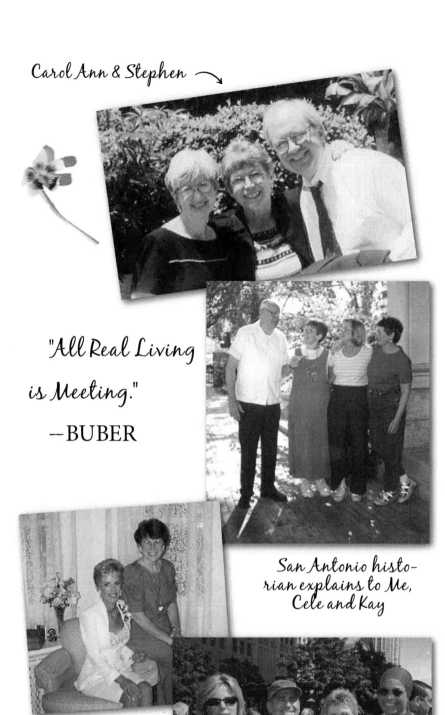

Carol Ann & Stephen

"All Real Living
is Meeting."
—BUBER

San Antonio histo-
rian explains to Me,
Cele and Kay

Bobbie,
mother of the bride

Chicago 9/11 Remembrance

244

There's always something to smile about when you have faith and friends.
— MARGARET

Aunt Kate & Abbot Claude

Buckstegge Cousins ↗
Arizona Reunion

Peifer
Cousins at
Jim and
Angie's

Reunion of St. Procopius Grads

Special people and pets

Sarah & Tiger

Julie & Scamper

Veronica goes camping

246

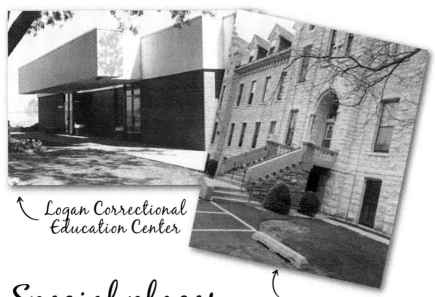

Logan Correctional
Education Center

Joliet Motherhouse
Now USF Wellness
Center

Thank
You
Jesus
Collages

Special places
in my life...

Peifer
Farm

Cindi's baby shower,
with Sherrie & Don,
and Jesse

Jack's cousins,
Colleen & Meghan

Lorette & I
choose card
winners

Collin and Adam Voyles, Men of Action

Thank You Jesus Collages

Nora and Stephen, children of Paula Uremovic Laskowski, Ph.D. SFA, 1970

February 16th, 1999 in Tucson - celebrating our 1st Anniversay with Sister Karen Berry (seated) and Sister Kathy Salewski (standing)

Thank you Jesus, Alleluia! Amen.

artpacks

Publishing, fine art printing, lifeprints, and studio workshops in book arts and life development. Contact us to learn more about our work or to order copies of *Nice To Meet Your Husband Sister Martha*.

artpacks
535 22nd Street NE
Rochester, Minnesota 55906

telephone 507·273·2529
virginiawoodruff@charter.net

Nice To Meet Your Husband Sister Martha, $39.00
Shipping is $3.50 for the first book, and $1 for each aditional copy.
Checks, Mastercard, and VISA accepted.

quantity
_____

shipping
_____

total
_____

Nice to Meet Your Husband Sister Martha is also available at

Prairie Years Book Store

121 North Kickapoo
Lincoln, Illinois 62656
telephone 217·732·6462
psheley@adi.org